MW01193693

Suffering ~ A Path of Awakening

Dissolving the Pain of Incest, Abuse, Addiction and Depression

Shellee Rae

Rae of Light Publishing

Ashland, Oregon

Suffering ~ A Path of Awakening

Dissolving the Pain of Incest, Abuse, Addiction and Depression

Second edition

ISBN: 978-1515161615

Library of Congress Number: 2009924075

Dedication

Dedicated to Tigger, who gave his life as the final thrust for my awakening.

Acknowledgements ~

Thank you Bob Valine (author of The Second Birth) for your time, encouragement, and helpful feedback during the writing of the book. Thank you Avram Novick for your superb editing skills and the gentle delivery of so many wonderful suggestions. Thank you Lou Goldberg for your many tireless reads of the manuscript and for your enthusiastic support. Thank you Saniel Bonder for your initial interest in my story and your encouragement to share its inspirational message with others. And thank you to the rest of my beautiful friends who read and gave feedback as the book was being born. You were all so very beneficial to its completion.

Foreword

"You're in for a Journey"

By Saniel Bonder

Shellee Rae first shared a draft of this little book with me about a year ago, I believe. Recently, when she asked and I immediately agreed to provide a brief foreword, she sent me a more complete manuscript. So I thought I'd just scan through it to remind myself of what she's gone through and where she lets you know she's come to.

Problem is, this book doesn't lend itself to being scanned through. I read out loud to my wife and teaching partner Linda just a couple of random paragraphs. She was astounded. "She really went through all *that?!*" I said, "That's just a few lines. The whole book's like this. The story just goes on and on." In the course of our work Linda and I have encountered many, many, many horror stories of abuse, addiction, madness, violence, and shock lying just under the surface of the lives of apparently sane, integrated, functional women, and men too. People participating in the daily affairs of the life around them, yet carrying vast reservoirs within them of memories of experiences that are virtually beyond the comprehension of others who've never gone through anything like that — never mind endless, relentless years and decades of it.

I have told Shellee, and I am happy to tell you, that I feel privileged, honored, in truth blessed, to have been able to be of service to her in her journey back — forward, actually, profoundly forward for the first time — to authentically sane life. She is truly a Wounded Heroine. Let her remarkably light-touch telling of this unbearably heavy story reveal to you an essential secret of life that you too can know as your own:

Nothing can defeat the human spirit unless we let it.

Nothing.

No matter how broken you've been, Shellee's authentic voice and story can help you heal — which means, become whole.

At the beginning Shellee tells us plainly that she's sharing her story so that those others of us who are like her, who have indeed been dragging through our whole lives the huge balls and chains of such devastation, can know that it is in fact possible to find light at the end of that tunnel.

And I have no doubt that even if you have never known such brokenness yourself, you're in for a revelation that will help you find compassion of a depth you've never been able to access before.

Whoever you are, you're in for a journey.

Blessings on your journey!

In the Beginning...

There is so much to tell, over such a great span of years that how much to tell and where to start this story have always been my problem. I know that it needs to be told, no, has to be told; it actually has an organic longing to be shared in hopes of inspiring and assisting others to emerge from the depths of their personal hells. My one great wish for you who are struggling is that you may find the courage to drag yourself along just a bit further because there is life after hell, I know, my life is proof of it.

For the most part, I guess I was amongst the *average* when I was a little girl. I had dreams and hopes, visions of magic and fairies, and thought that I might like to be a doctor or a movie-star when I grew up (both such prestigious, high income positions!). I had an older brother and a younger sister and brother. We played, dreamed, looked out for each other and fought as brothers and sisters do. Our family moved a lot and as a young girl, I never understood why. It was torturous saying good-bye and having to leave my friends behind over and over again.

Looking back, it seems like an old, faded, black & white movie of someone else's life – hard to believe it was mine, especially given where I am today; a healthy woman in wonderful relationships; a mother of two beautiful, respectable, grown children; a compassionate, spiritual, awakened being working and living in a place where I finally feel like I fit. Back then, I never expected to live to thirty – nor did I want to.

I don't remember much about my life before nine years of age. I do remember feeling at times that the world seemed overwhelming to me and it didn't make any sense at all. I couldn't understand the tug in my heart for something more. I used to hold my breath until I fainted – it was such a great relief to slip out of this reality even if it was only temporary. I liked the escape and I loved the whole body buzz I felt upon awakening. I also got a lot of attention from family and friends when I did it. The headache I would get afterwards was brutal but that did not stop me from doing it again and again. I don't know what the initial trigger was that caused me to want to check out but I suspect it closely resembled the deep longing to *not be here* or to *go home* that I've experienced all my life.

I think I loved my parents, although the fighting and arguing was always scary. We never knew what would happen; a plate of flying spaghetti, someone knocked out of their chair, a backhand or knuckles from nowhere, etc. My father even left for a year when I was seven. I found out much later that he had run off to California with his secretary. Life was rarely dull. The atmosphere definitely taught me to be on guard and alert at all times! Even with fear of the unknown, I thought my parents to be the most beautiful people I knew. My mother was a lovely goddess and my father was the most handsome and funny man on the planet.

Life has a way of throwing a wrench into the works from time to time and the world that I had become accustomed to (uncomfortable as it was) completely shattered when I was nine years old.

The Wrench...

I was born on January 4th, 1960 in Saint Petersburg, Florida. After living in many homes and a few different states, in 1969 we moved to Perkinsville, Vermont. I remember the first frost (we thought it was snow); we grabbed some wide strips of cardboard and ran across the street to our neighbors hilly yard and had our first slide of the season, pretty much destroying their grass.

It was exciting being up north and seeing all that snow when the real thing finally did come. We got toboggans and sleds for Christmas and we did not waste any time getting out and discovering the joy of sliding down the slopes. My parents had found a trail and we packed up for an adventure. Not knowing that it was a bit bumpy and fast for us novices, we mounted our snow vehicles and took to the trail. I don't remember how many times or how many of us crashed but the grand finale was my mother flying over a mogul and breaking her tailbone. That was the beginning of the end of life as I knew it.

That evening we were all a bit stiff and sore from our bumpy day out in the wild. My father asked if I could rub his shoulders and neck to help relieve him of his aches and pains. I of course, happily did so and with gusto because, being a Capricorn, that is what we do – I put my heart, hands and soul into helping my father feel better. He was grateful, praised me for a good job and said he felt better.

Because my mother couldn't get down the cellar stairs, I stayed up late *that* night to finish the laundry. For her comfort, she was set up in the living room to sleep on the couch (I imagine on some pretty good pain medication too). We lived in a small four-room duplex that had only two bedrooms. All four kids had to pass through my parent's bedroom to get to our room, which was divided with a curtain in the middle of the room – girls bunks on one side and boys on the other.

I was the last one in *that* night due to helping with the chores that my mother couldn't accomplish. Tired and passing through my parent's room, my father quietly asked if I could give him another massage. I didn't know why I felt fear. I didn't know why I wanted to say no. There was something different this time in his request and I froze. I whispered that I was really tired and just wanted to go to bed. He assured me that he only wanted a couple more minutes of my wonderful massage expertise. I dragged my feet to the side of his bed. As I started rubbing his shoulders and he started grabbing at my panties from under my nightgown, white-hot-lightening-bolts were going off in my mind. Then a strange thing happened, I went from frantic-horror, shaking, crying and totally freaking out, to concentrated focus on where he was stuffing my panties – at the very edge, between the mattress and boxspring – my only thought was, I have to get my panties, I have to get my panties… I think it was the beginning of a quite helpful survival skill, disassociation, which I took into my adult years.

The life I knew was over. Nothing was ever the same. All trust had been destroyed. Betrayal seemed such a tiny and incredibly inadequate word for what I was feeling. Five years in a stupor of sexual abuse, physical beatings and other assorted inappropriate events passed at the speed of what seemed like frozen-time.

On the Run...

My father was an active alcoholic and I recall my mother's drinking becoming much more frequent by the time I was twelve, "Shh, for medicinal reasons only", she used to whisper when I'd catch her slamming down a double shot of vodka in the kitchen and chasing it with a glass of Tab. I swore that I would never be at all like either of my parents.

My mother also took pills to ease the pain of her life. She knew that my father was running around with other women but she simply could not leave him and swears to this day that she had no idea he was having his way with me too. There were some pretty huge sign-posts for her but when one's world is in a flux of constant chaos, I can see how things might be missed or misinterpreted. However, if my daughter had insomnia, was seen sleeping with her eyes open, dealing with chronic constipation, stomach problems (an ulcer that wasn't diagnosed until I was seventeen) and was running away from home, I'd be doing some serious investigating. But then my mother certainly had her own demons to struggle with. I witnessed a couple of her suicide attempts.

I was only a year old for my mother's first suicide attempt but somehow, cellularly, something remembers. I finally asked her some years ago if she tried to take her life while she was pregnant with me and that's when she told me the story of her first attempt when she was pregnant with my sister. I was twelve years old for her second suicide attempt. What a freak show – I mean like freaky-scary and just plain surreal. I do not recollect what the recent eruption was about, there were so many of them, but I do remember a lot of yelling, physical struggling and tears. My mother disappeared from the scene and all got quiet. I guess my father eventually went to see if she was okay and found the bathroom door locked, that's when the real drama began. He knocked and yelled and banged and demanded that she open the door – all to no avail. Then came the big bang and a whole new world was created – he kicked the door in and came running down the stairs with a rag-doll figure of my mother in his arms. He was shoving his fingers down her throat and yelling at her to stay awake!

How did I slip into this dimension and more importantly, where is the portal back to my world?

I don't recall who called the emergency room to let them know we were coming but I do know that my father was not waiting around for any ambulance. The whole way there he kept yelling at me to keep my mother awake, "Keep slapping her in the face!" he'd scream.

Holy shit, I thought…my mother is fucking dying and you want me to hit her?!

All focus was on my mother and I have no idea where my brothers or sister were at this point or what they were experiencing. Did they stay at home or were they right there in the car? I couldn't see anything but

11

my mother's eyes rolling back in her head and the foam coming out of her mouth.

The paramedics were in receiving mode when we arrived at the hospital and they went right to work on her. She was in a coma for a long time (ten days as I recall) and the doctors said that if she did come out of it, she would never be the same because her brain was too damaged. We all kept going in and visiting her, talking about daily routine things trying to get her to snap out of it. We'd say things like, 'we missed the bus and need a ride to school' and 'I need help with my homework' and 'wake up Mom, it's time to put the coffee on' and other everyday phrases – it seemed crazy to us at the time but the doctor assured us that on some level she could hear us. I kept having the thought that 'there is no way in hell this woman is going to die and leave me alone with *him*'; I absolutely would not stand for it and I told her so in many ways. She did finally come out of the coma and it was as if she were waking up to start the day as usual. Very gratefully her brain cells were still functioning and all went back to *normal* within a short period of time.

We never lived anywhere much more than a year. I think my father was trying to outrun his pain and shame, probably the law too. He certainly would have been behind bars if the things that he was doing behind closed doors leaked out. Oh how I loathed him. I used to fantasize ways to kill him – ways that would look like an accident. Frequently, I was used as his personal bartender and I wished with all my heart that I could get my hands on some untraceable poison that would take him slowly and then finish him off after he passed out. If not that, at least get him good and soused with a heavy-handed-pour, so that he would sleep through the night!

God was on my loathing list too. *He* had never done anything for me that was worth honoring *Him* for. My father sang in the church choir for God's sake! His father was a minister who was also an abusive alcoholic and sexually suggestive with me and one of

13

my girlfriends – I don't have much more history on him except that my father and his two siblings spent three years in an orphanage because of the abuse that was going on at home. If there was a God, I wasn't interested in doing business with *Him*.

Nothing made sense to me – all the pain and suffering and injustice in the world – what's up with that God, huh?

It all seemed so horribly wrong! Sitting in church made me feel like I was either going to throw up or perhaps spontaneously combust and what made it even more uncomfortable was the feeling of pride that pushed its way into my heart when my father's voice was the loudest and most pristine in the choir. Seeing him up there smiling and singing stirred feelings of confusion, anger, hatred and anxiety deep within my being.

He beat and sexually abused me into my teen years until I finally outed him at age fourteen. Not long

14

after that, I moved in with my boyfriend and his family.

The deeper that sorrow carves into your being the more joy you can contain. Is not the cup that holds your wine the very cup that was burned in the potter's oven? ~ Kahlil Gibran

You may be wondering why, oh why didn't I tell on my father sooner! I know I would be. He threatened me. I was a young child and I believed his threats. He said if I made noise and woke my sister he'd have to do it to her too. He hinted that he might have to kill us all. He promised me that my mother would never believe it and that I would probably be sent to reform school for telling such sick lies about him.

He was right too, my mother didn't believe me – at first.

My father was in Reno on a *business trip* (he had women all over the place so who knows what was really going on) when I got caught doing my Christmas shoplifting and was in big trouble. I was in one store while my mother was grocery shopping in another. Geez, there was nobody around and the picking was easy. I had no idea about store surveillance cameras. While casually strolling out of the store with that 'I didn't find what I was looking for' look on my face, security grabbed me.

Now there's a rush.

They asked that I join them in the back office to talk about the things I had stolen. My heart moved into my throat and my stomach took its place while we walked the long mile to the back room.

The seams in my coat pockets (which were full of jewelry) were weak and I was able to pop through with my fingers, ripping them open. I stuffed the jewels in the front of my pants (well, actually right into my underwear – who's going to look there?) while the whole abracadabra was hidden by my coat. When we were all in behind closed doors, I did as they asked and emptied all my pockets. Clean. Then I emptied my purse. Oops, cigarettes, toker-stone, papers and a small bag of weed but none of which they were interested in. They then said that they had it on camera and I could come out with the goods on my own or they could call in the police for a strip search.

Holy Cow! Is that legal?

I wasn't willing to gamble so I reached into my pants and dropped the goods, pubic hair and all, on the desk in front of me. They paged my mother and my world began to shift again. She arrived, white as a ghost and had to use the wall to hold herself up.

Damn I didn't mean to hurt her, why was she always getting in the line of fire?

House arrest and six months' probation were the penalties but the higher price I might have to pay was the threat [from my parents] of reform school…now where had I heard that before?

That's when I spilled the beans. I no longer cared if Dad did it to my sister; I no longer cared if Mom didn't believe me; I no longer cared if he killed us all; I no longer cared about anything. I was tired. The problem was that I had been such a *problem child* for so long that my mother thought it was just one more of my dramas. I had run away from home two times at that point and participated in various other parent-worrying activities. She *didn't* believe me. She said that we would have a talk with my father when he got home. Oh man! It wasn't unfolding at all like I planned. I figured we'd all be packed and gone by the time he got back.

He arrived, knowing the details of what happened at the store and then Mom took him aside and told him of my accusations. He denied it vehemently and they had me come join them in their room.

Can people die of fear?

As he denied it, I met his gaze, thought of ripping his eyes out, began crying and he cracked. He admitted it all and promised to get help – which never happened.

Let the Numbing Begin...

I had my first alcohol blackout when I was eleven

> *"By choosing not to allow parts of ourselves to exist, we are forced to expend huge amounts of psychic energy to keep them beneath the surface."* ~ Debbie Ford

years old. My sister and I had a friend sleep over; we camped in a tent in the edge of the woods of our backyard. The parents were out and we mixed a killer cocktail – about an inch of booze from every bottle to fill a tall tumbler. It was enough to get the three of us good and drunk. I do not remember what happened soon after the drinking began. I thought my sister threw up but they said it was me. We blamed it on the dog.

That was the start to my *anything-but-this-feeling* career, and that is what it was – work! It was work to not get caught nipping away at the alcohol; it was work to plan on how to get more; it was work to constantly be on the lookout for an opportunity to get alcohol or drugs, whether at friends' houses, school or work. Stealing from the homes that I worked in babysitting or cleaning was always a good source but I did get caught from time to time. I worked very hard to not feel what was going on in my life. My motto was "reality is for those who can't handle their booze". Little did I know that I wasn't handling the alcohol (or drugs) very well at all!

I began occasionally huffing gas when I was nine years old and smoking cigarettes when I was ten. By the ripe old age of twelve, I was smoking pot, hash and opium, taking speed regularly, drinking as often as I could and having sex with my boyfriends. My father grew his own marijuana and I could always find his stash. I freely helped myself to it figuring, hey, what the hell's he going to say, "Who's been stealing my pot?"

By the time I was fourteen, I had permission to drink and smoke in the house. Although my mother didn't smoke much pot, she was the master roller – she could

21

roll a joint like no one else. We had parties at our house. My father would buy the beer and he always had a stash of Mom's superbly rolled joints to share. I had girlfriends who were in love with my father and we had friends who wanted to move in with us. So what was I so depressed about? Why was I sick all the time? The gut-wrenching torture of having to hide his sickness and my misery felt like it was killing me.

There were many times that I was reprimanded for crying for *no reason*. Oh how I hated hearing "Stop that crying or I'll give you something to cry about!" I simply wanted to scream to her about what Dad was doing to me but the words would not come out. "Wait until your father gets home!" was another of my favorites – as if I didn't already wish that he weren't coming home and like one more whipping was going to matter at all.

Yes, they had a whip, it was a homemade cat o'nine tails. I remember watching in horror as my mother was putting it together (just when I thought it couldn't

22

get any worse). She had an old wide leather strap that she cut in half and then cut into nine strips. She used fishing line (catgut she called it – how appropriate I thought for a cat o'nine tails); carefully and very tightly she wrapped and wrapped the line around a wooden handle that she had sandwiched the leather in. Voila. A new torture tool, yeah. I was already too familiar with the old ones – switches, extension cords, hands (to include knuckles and fingernails), rulers and other assorted household items – I was not looking forward to experiencing the new one.

Often, when something would happen, (a broken *something*, missing money, etc.), we were interrogated in a line-up and if the guilty party did not step forward, we would all get a whipping. There could be no ratting either – even when we knew who the culprit was – the guilty party would have to confess themselves. Many times, either I or my older brother would step forward and take the unjustified beating to save the violence on three others, especially the tender skin of our youngest brother.

My father got off on having me pull my pants down most of the time for my whippings. I still don't know if my siblings got the same treatment and none of them were sexually abused as far as they recall. One time, I had padded myself not expecting the strip down (the crime was minor) and got caught. After that, it was 'down to the bare skin little missy' every time. I could sometimes bring up enough anger to not even cry – I hated him so – and that would somehow make me feel just a little better, showing him that he could not make me cry no matter how hard he hit me.

Weird twisted worlds upon twisted worlds, sporadically my father would give me the option of receiving a real live whipping or would offer the animated version – he would whip the bed and I would scream and cry as if I were really being hit. I think he did this to soothe his guilt at times or maybe to try and create more of a *secret bond* between us but either way, both created deep emotional scars.

Ultimately, he would almost always come to my room

and apologize, saying how much he loved me and how much he hated having to punish me. I hated it when he asked me, "You still love your daddy don't you?" I wanted to puke. My mind screamed 'I hate you!' but my lips quivered out a 'yes'. I could not imagine the punishment I would receive if I were ever to tell him what I was really feeling. Sometimes as an extra bestowment to show his remorse, he would promise to leave me alone for a designated number of nights – now that was worth something.

I did discover that a few of those pills from the medicine cabinet or even simply a hand full of aspirin would help take the edge off of my tortured existence.

I wish I could remember some of the more enjoyable and cheery experiences of my life but it all seems so overshadowed with hurt and dysfunction. I know that we went ice skating, skiing, to carnivals, Disney Land, and lots of other family events but they don't seem to have much of an influence on my memory. Someone once said to me, "I'm not going to remember you as

much by what you say but by how you make me feel."
To take that theory a step further, I think the stronger
the feeling, the bigger the impact it has on the memory
and the greater its power of overshadowing everything
else.

If you question any one of my siblings, they had such
a different experience of our upbringing that one
would think we came from different homes.
Periodically, one of them will be talking about some
place that we went or something that we all did and I
will be sitting there in the dark, having no idea what
they are talking about. Occasionally someone will
enthusiastically ask me, "Remember that?" and I can
only answer with a blank-faced no.

One particular evening of reminiscing brought us back
to a favorite restaurant of Dad's and how cool it was
that we got to go into the lounge with the parents
afterwards; they shared the wine with us and we all got
to dance. The "cool" I remember was the smoothness
of my father's moves that no one else could see while I

was on the dance floor with him. My dance with him (even though I didn't want to) stirred feelings of hatred and longing – a longing to be able to let go and feel safe and loved in the fierce protectiveness of a father's arms, something that I desperately wished for.

I always thought that my childhood was the reason I never seemed to FIT anywhere. In later years, I tried the corporate world (and ten other careers over time) and nothing ever felt right for me nor did it soothe that inner longing and gnawing ache at the core of my being. Drugs and alcohol (mostly alcohol) became my salve but I will get to that in a minute.

Thrills and Spills...

Along with drugs and alcohol, I loved the adrenaline rush that came from things that put my body in fear. The fastest ride at the carnival, smoking in the girl's bathroom in school, smoking pot in the smoking area (got caught a couple of times but for the most part was pretty ingenious about it), skipping school, getting into bars under age, driving before getting my license, blasting around on the snowmobile and riding motorcycles were only a few of the ways that I got my thrills.

I owned my first motorcycle when I was twelve years old and I loved racing my older brother and pushing myself beyond the limits of fear. I took a few spills but six motorcycles and thirty-seven years later, I'm still walking and talking about it.

However, driving drunk, hung-over or in a blackout with an addiction to driving fast caused many a fender-

bender. The world was my enabler and somehow I
always managed to come out of the mess without
much retribution. It's odd thinking back on all the
close-calls and the more serious accidents; I don't
know how I lived through some of them.

I skipped school many, many times and that in and of
itself was a big enough rush for me but some of the
things that happened while out and about always made
it juicier. I remember one time I had my best friend on
the back of my motorcycle which was not road
registered but had a fake plate. There were two clubs
in town that would serve us and we were on our way
to one of them, a bar at the beach (we were fourteen).
We got a flat tire half way there. The first rush was
that we didn't die (you know what I am talking about
if you have ever experienced a flat on a motorcycle)
and the second was, 'how are we going to get our butts
and the bike home in time to show up as if we were
just strolling in from school?' Cocktails at this
particular point were no longer a priority. As fate
would have it, a friend with a pickup just happened to

29

be passing by and gave us – bike and all – a ride back to the safety zone…cocktails all the way.

Another time with the same friend, we were skipping school again and thumbing into town (where life was so much more exciting). We had all kinds of plans for the day – none of them good but what fun! So there we were strolling on a happy high down the street with our thumbs out and my friend started to get a funny look on her face – her eyebrows furrowed together and squinting – then her airborne thumb slowly began wilting. I couldn't imagine what was happening and she whispered barely audibly, "I think that's my father coming."

Holy bazookas batman! This just doesn't happen in real life!

He pulled up to us, calmly said, "Get in" and we rode in shock back to the house. He was a cop – yep, a real live copper and we got nabbed. We were not allowed to talk on the phone or see each other for a whole

30

month but thank the powers that be, he promised not to tell my parents – he knew the potential of pain that could cause me.

That being said, I did tell a couple of people (without getting into much detail) about my father before I told my mother. My school-skipping friend was one, who then told her mother, who then told her husband, who was a policeman and nothing happened, except that he didn't blow the whistle on me to my father about us ditching school. The first one was my school guidance counselor when I was twelve; he gently patted my knee and said that I needed to talk to my mother about that. It felt like this was something that he did not want to take on and the simpler solution would be to just sweep me under the rug. Done.

I had experienced enough signs of trouble in my teens that someone else – not alcoholic – would spot right away and say, "Eww, that's a red flag", but not an alcoholic. I had my first car accident when I was twelve, no one was hurt but I almost lost my boyfriend's car in the Ottoquechee River. Thank goodness for the pickup truck driver with chains who came around the corner and helped us out, he was also as stoned as we were.

I had another bad car accident when I was sixteen (skipping the last day of school before Christmas vacation and coming back from a party). There were five of us in the car and two of us ended up in the hospital, me with stitches in my face and my best friend with a broken collarbone and crushed ankle. Odd that the sixth person in the vehicle was dropped off at the bottom of the mountain – if he'd been in the car, he would have been crushed and perhaps killed where he was sitting – odd because two years later while driving drunk, he was responsible for the death of a family of four. Bizarre to me that it wasn't meant for me to kill him in my accident but that he was meant to live to kill this man and woman and their two children.

Who's in charge of this drama anyway?

Like-energy attracts like-energy. Our family was lost in chaos and lived in crisis-mode, so we attracted a lot of chaos to us. My friend with the ankle and collarbone injury while in her wheelchair and I still with stitches in my face joined my parents and other siblings (all under-age) at a bar for our New Year's Eve celebration. We all got pretty tanked up drinking mostly MD 20/20 (egads!) and at the end of the night my parents headed for home while we kids headed off to a party. I don't remember exactly how it was discovered (police scanner radio I think) but a friend announced to me and my siblings that on the way home from the bar, my parents got into a head-on collision and were both in the hospital.

Will somebody please pinch me because I'm ready to wake up from this nightmare!

My father was thrown through the windshield while my mother was taken out with the jaws-of-life (the thing can take the roof off a car in about two minutes!). He thought she was dead and she thought he was dead. The doctors didn't allow them to see each other for fear of the shock it might cause – my father was cut up pretty badly and my mother was pretty broken. When we all came to visit them, Mom and Dad thought we were lying to them about the other being alive – to give them the strength to hold on. Mom's punctured lungs filled with fluid and she slipped away. When they revived her, she told the doctors that if he was alive she demanded to see him – they brought him in right away and that relieved the fear for both of them. His recovery was much faster and less painful than hers. She had a broken pelvis (and many other broken bones), and she had to learn how to walk again.

The driver that they collided with had four DUI's.

Not long after that event, I was on my motorcycle and my younger brother was a couple of cars behind me where he witnessed one of my accidents. A car came out of a one-way street going the wrong way and I didn't see him until it was too late (mind you, I was hung-over). I hit my brakes and crashed into the car broadside, flew over the car while the bike went under and I slid and slid before landing up against the curb. My brother saw a flying body, feared the worst and was right, it was me. I suffered some nerve injury and had to wear a neck brace and an arm immobilizer for a while. I went to visit my mother to show her the new bike that the insurance company had recently paid for, while still in the neck brace. Poor Mom.

Another time I discovered my motorcycle on its side in the front lawn of my apartment in a circle of dead grass from all the gas leaking out and not remembering how it got there. That's when I made the decision to be safe and take the car when I knew I'd be drinking. The thought to not drink didn't even cross my mind. I guess someone else might have seen it as the proverbial red flag to a possible alcohol problem. Hmm. I never said that I was very sharp back then – the solution seemed to make sense to me at the time.

One of the worst accidents I survived was when I was t

hrown through the rear window of a car at approximately 100 mph. Coming back from a club, I was a (drunk) passenger in the back seat of my roommate's car. He was trying to impress his friend with the amazing speed of his brand new Cougar. Burying the needle of the speedometer, he lost control while passing a vehicle when another car pulled into our lane. I lost count at how many 360's we did before we hit a tree with the rear-end of the car which catapulted me through the rear windshield. Flying through glass and trees, my clothes were torn, I was bleeding from many places and just the strap to one shoe was left on my ankle when I finally landed about 50 feet from the car. It was around 2 AM and I recall hearing voices calling my name and I could see flashlights combing the woods; I thought I was yelling back to them but no one was responding to my call. I could see my body lying there and not moving. I had the thought of "Hmm, so this is what it's like to be dead; it doesn't hurt at all. I feel fine, better than that I feel free!"

My sister was the one who eventually found me. She was coming back from the same club with a breakfast stop in between. As she and her friend were nearing the site of the accident, she screamed, "Stop, that's my sister!" All she saw was the glint of a cougar on the hood of the car in the woods and somehow she knew it was me.

Once the state police arrived, they were talking about me as if I couldn't hear them, commenting on how bad it was and openly making suggestive remarks about my half-naked, shapely body. One officer nudged the other while nodding in my direction and said, "Not bad, huh?" My roommate was standing beside him at that point and told the officer to "shut the fuck up". Weirdly, again, I could hear myself telling him to be careful about what he was saying because he was drunk and probably in deep trouble. However, still watching myself lying there, I could hear my voice but my lips were not moving at all and no one was responding to my words.

The paramedics took over; the emergency moved to the hospital; I woke up back in my body stitched up, taped up, propped up and then convalesced for 3 months.

I wondered at that point how many lives I had left.

"Many of us are frightened to look within ourselves, and fear has us put up walls so thick we no longer remember who we really are." ~ Debbie Ford

I graduated a year early from high school (don't ask me how!) doubling up on classes and cheating a bit. School was really a bother, boring and totally getting in the way of the more important things in life, if I could only figure out what those *things* were.

Most everything I tried felt pretty good for a while but with each new thing the thrill grew shorter and the hunt more desperate. Looking on the outside to fix my insides, I went from one home, state, job and relationship to the next while never quenching that thirst for deeper meaning in my life. It was as if I had

38

a beast within me who had an insatiable appetite for more and the deeper dilemma was 'how to kill the beast'.

Part of my longing to fit expressed itself through the meandering I did in many work arenas. I got my first job when I was eleven years old, a relatively regular babysitting gig. To increase my revenue, I became the attendant of the information booth at the Quechee Gorge in Vermont, (my father had some *inside connections* – who knows what that meant – and got me the job). From there I wandered through brief stints as a chambermaid, department store clerk, hairdresser or rather 'beauty-school-dropout', short-order cook, model-wanna-be, waitress and bartender (when do doctor or movie-star come in?), heavy equipment operator/truck driver and then a fork-lift operator on the dock of a large computer company. While there, I dabbled in the paperwork end of shipping and receiving, creating a more organized filing system (I'm Capricorn you know!), then bulldozed my way into an office job out amongst the techies, managing the import/export documentation procedures and wearing 'executive-type clothing'.

All were so proud of me as I had finally *made it* but it was torturous living in this world that had no real meaning to me. Three years later I moved from that computer company to another doing similar type of work but adding duty-drawback as my main responsibility, which meant I was working with Customs and a Customs Broker to help the company receive their duty back (in case you are wondering… U.S. Customs law allows manufacturers to recover ninety-nine percent of the duties paid on imported goods that are used to manufacture U.S. products for export). I got laid off from that company (six months pregnant -- more later on that), and continued for a while consulting, using a broker and attempting to keep my foot in the executive-world. So that I didn't have to pay a *middle-man*, I studied, paid the $1,000 entry fee, went for the big Customs Broker exam – BIG – and had such a hangover that day that I could barely read English; I failed.

I stumbled into another field in the computer world through temp agencies, while on the side I was teaching myself how to get around in a database, create spreadsheets and templates, etc. so I was able to pick up some contract jobs. It all seemed pretty mundane and meaningless to me but it helped to pay the bills and I had alcohol to numb the gnaw. Because dying would be a great relief and it didn't look like that was going to happen anytime too soon, my mantra was 'life sucks and then you live' – how prophetic really, looking at it now.

Guns and Guidance...

My father committed suicide when I was 20. Mom never did leave him. Because of his behavior and her suicide attempts she was afraid we kids would all end up in foster care. Fear. It is such a paralyzer.

The event of my father's suicide was just another strange and surreal episode in my world. My parents were out on the lake in their boat and they had a fight. He was in an alcohol blackout and might have beaten the life out of her if she did not get away. They were docked by then and she ran and hid in someone else's boat, bleeding all over the place (I can imagine the look on that boat-owners face when the mess was discovered). Once the coast was clear (literally), she walked five miles to the hospital – I guess people were afraid to stop and offer a ride to someone looking like she did, all torn and covered in blood. They sewed her face up in the ER and the call came for a ride home. My sister and I were living in a farmhouse with six other people and even though I wanted to go, the vote was for my sister to go get Mom and deliver her home. My boyfriend had to hold me down and babysit me to keep me from going out and finding my father – I was going to kill him, no doubt in my mind!

The next morning I phoned my mother to see how she was doing. She was flat, no life in her voice at all. I asked if Dad was home and she said he had not come home all night. Charge! I hopped in my car and drove to their house as fast as I could. I told her that my boyfriend's parents (who lived in the western part of the state) were counselors and could help her and I would be happy to drive her over to meet them if she wanted to go. She dully responded with, "I'll just get my purse." My mother, who questions everything, did not ask how long we would be gone or how far it was, just said that she'd get her purse – even that didn't feel like it was happening fast enough because I knew if my father showed up that the whole scene would change very quickly. My heart felt like it was going to beat right out of my chest!

We drove for two hours in almost complete silence. My mouth was so dry that I do not think I could have spoken even if I wanted to. The adrenaline-hit had caused a case of dry mouth like I'd just crawled out of the desert. I couldn't help but keep glancing at her – like a train wreck ya know – I didn't want to keep looking but I couldn't stop my eyes from wandering back to her. At a very deep level I sensed that our world had just been completely altered by what we were doing.

My boyfriend, Gregg, called his parents to let them know we were coming and they set up the guest room for us. No one was supposed to let my father know where she was nor was he to have the phone number. Mom went into counseling and Dad was given some recommendations for a therapist in his area. Within a couple of weeks they were supposed to have a joint session but only if my father got started on his end.

I don't remember how long we were there, it may have been one week or it could have been three, every day blurred into the next. Mom did call and speak to Dad briefly a couple of times against her therapist's advice. She said that he really wanted to see her and that he was sorry (how many times had we all heard that?) and she thought she might like to talk to him face to face. I told her I would take her if that was what she really wanted.

That night I had a dream, well actually like two dreams fuzzing into each other. Leaving out the unimportant details, part one of the dream: my mother had changed her mind and decided not to go see my father and he killed himself ~~fuzz into part two~~ I took my mother back to their house and my father killed her and then killed himself. I recall feeling great fear about whether or not I should share the dream with her; if I told her and she did not go home because of that information and he killed himself, I could take a big hit for that. I might get blamed for interfering or she might always wonder if she had been there whether she could have stopped him, and I might always question if I had done the right thing by sharing it with her. If I did not tell her and he killed her too, I would never forgive myself for not sharing the foreboding dream. I was so grateful when my mother told me the next day that she had decided not to go back. I then told her about the dream.

So now I had this feeling that my father was going to shoot himself. My youngest brother (sixteen) was still living at home and I told him he had to get all the guns out of the house – what a good kid – he loaded them up in his trunk and stashed them at the farm where my sister and I were living with many other people.

Oh thank God.

My father discovered that the guns were gone and said that he wanted them back home, telling my brother that it was illegal for them to be in the hands of someone not licensed for them. "Besides", he laughed, "what do you think I'm going to do, shoot someone?" Obedient son that he was and knowing where they were, he came and got the guns while we were out and gave them back to my father.

Soon thereafter, being the greatest con of cons and with a silver tongue, my father got the phone number and the address where my mother and I were staying from my brother. He told my brother that Mom needed him to come right away and to bring a few things. Chivalry was not dead, my brother immediately hopped in the car and headed our way.

The phone rang and I answered. Jesus, it was him.

How did he get this number and where is he!?

My heart froze and I was shaking like a leaf; something big was about to go down – I could feel it. He hammered me with a few questions, then told me that I don't know *everything* and said to put Mom on.

I guess my boyfriend's father, Gene, saw the blood drain from my face because he grabbed the phone from me. I sat back down at the table and kept staring at my macaroni and cheese wondering if the little bit that I had already eaten was going to stay down or not. Dad yelled at him for a bit, said he knew what the hell was going on – hanky-panky-bullshit – and then he pulled the trigger.

No fucking way. I saw it happen in his face – it was now Gene's turn for the blood to drain from his face. Without a word he hung up the phone, lifted the phone, hung up the phone and ran next door. Since apparently the phone was still off the hook on my father's end, he needed a phone that he could get a dial-tone on to call the police.

Not that any one person would be better than another to be on the receiving end of the phone when something like that happens but of all the people for it to happen to – at the age of fourteen, Gene, who had been shot and was thought to be dead, witnessed the murder of his whole family by his father who then turned the gun on himself – Gene was the only survivor.

The rest of that night is a blur; the police broke into my parent's house and confirmed that yes, he was definitely dead – 308 rifle will be sure to get the job done. He had poured out all of his alcohol and apparently not had a drink in a few days (detoxing I'm sure!), had the bible open on the bed next to him and left a six-page letter to my mother that I have not been allowed to read, and one page to me:

"Dear Shel,
Sorry.
Love,
Dad"

Balls man – big ones. If he were still alive I probably would have shot him myself I was so angry. What a cowardly thing to do! Mom said that he loved us all so dearly and that was his way to set us free. While that may have been what he said in her letter and even what he thought at the time, the deeper truth from my view was that he wanted to set himself free. I had all my judgments and angry feelings about the incident at the time. They morphed into sadness and compassion many years later.

I suppose we all had our feelings about the event. Close to two hours after Dad's exit, my sister showed up and greeted me on the stairs with a cold hard slap across the face saying that it was all my fault; that if I had not interfered in their lives he would still be here. I had a flash thought of, "Who here besides you wishes Dad were still here?" but kept my mouth shut.

My older brother, through a number of other circumstances which had left him with a very heavy heart had decided to move back to our home state of Florida and start a new life. He was on the road and was not immediately reachable when Dad died. Cells phone were a rare luxury in 1980.

Like me, my brother was sensitive. As kids, he and I used to talk for hours about the workings of the universe and what it all meant. We never could make any sense of it. He had great love and great fear of my

50

father, much like our family dog Radar who would come running to the door to greet my father with his tail wagging madly between his legs while leaving a trail of pee.

When my brother arrived at our aunt's house in Florida, she said he was needed at home, that our dad had just died and handed him an airline ticket home. He came back a different person with eyes as big as saucers and talking to beings that only he could see. He also said that the government knew that he *knew* their little secrets and that the CIA and maybe the FBI too were after him. He has been medicated and in a VA home ever since. Okay, now that broke my heart.

I cannot help but wonder why when this type of "illness" hits, that so many people have the same *delusions*. I tend to think that it is a filter problem and that they are too tapped into the infinite realm of information. He has shared some quite amazing details with me about some pretty esoteric and scientific things and I have no idea where he could have learned them. I have asked him in the past where he learns these things and he once answered, "If I told you Shellee, you would think I'm crazy." I said everyone thinks you're crazy anyway (we had a good laugh), he then said, "The spacemen teach me." I have no doubt.

Anyway, until my recent move across the country, I had always stayed close enough to visit him often. He's a great guy, funny and has a huge heart but I have carried a sadness all these years for the loss of the brother I knew.

Immediately after Dad's death, Mom and I both moved to the town in western Massachusetts where we had been staying, she to continue with her counseling and I to look after her until she got her land legs. I stayed for a year. My mother had not worked (except for a couple of brief jobs) in twenty-five years, not because she didn't want to necessarily but because my father would not allow it. She felt a little intimidated about jumping into the working world (not to say that raising four kids isn't work) but she got a job and soon enough slipped into the *grind*.

Getting her settled into a little apartment and her new life, with the help of many people, went as smoothly as one could expect I guess, given all the circumstances. Going through the items that came out of my parent's bedroom before delivering them to Mom was a real hair-raising experience. When I volunteered to help with the project, (having no prior experience of what happens in a room where someone's head has been blown off), I had no idea what I was in for. My boyfriend stepped in to take over when I was not able to finish the task. Completion of the move got a little delayed in the end, since finding a house cleaner who would 'do the job' was not an easy undertaking.

Who did he think was going to clean up that mess anyway?

I wish I could tell you that my life smoothed out and

became a peaceful ride once my father was gone but that was not the case; there were more trials and tribulations! Soon after Dad's death, Mom began working with an attorney to see if there was a way to collect on his $100,000 life insurance policy. The lawyer found a loop-hole in the suicide-clause. The suicide clause states that the policy is null and void if the insured person takes their own life. However, there was something in the policy that read "...being of right mind..." and my mother's tenacious lawyer with sound evidence was going to prove to the insurance company and the jury that suicide was not a "right mind" state. That is where the battle began. I was summoned as a witness.

I would like to say here on my mother's behalf that I was given the choice of her dropping the lawsuit and forgetting about the money. She did mention that she would not pursue the court case if testifying was something I felt I could not do. After all the years of hell and insanity, it just didn't seem right that Dad was leaving her with nothing but a shattered life and an empty bank account. I agreed to testify but had no idea what I was in for.

I cannot begin to tell you what it felt like to be cross-examined by heartless bastards whose job it was to make me look either crazy or like a liar to the jury.

Shouldn't there be some kind of line drawn to protect the already extremely injured!? What the hell kind of people are we becoming anyway?

After grilling me for specific incidents and demanding all the dirty little details, I felt naked and molested in front of all those people. I do not recall how my stripped, sobbing, shaking and nauseous body stepped down from the stand but I feel certain I was assisted. I wished I could die. In the end, she won. Case closed.

I've always had a fear of guns and it's no wonder, I've had so many chilling experiences with them. Being born in the south, there were more people who carried them than not. Whenever there was an incident, the gun got *drawn*. We had 'peeping toms' and other crazy crap always going on around us and when the gun surfaced, my heart stopped.

My father bought a .222 bolt action rifle that was eventually given to me and when I was twelve he wanted me to go hunting with him. He loved to shoot his guns and went hunting a lot, sometimes without even leaving the comfort of his own home. The image of my father sitting with the barrel of a gun poking out of his bedroom window, waiting for an unsuspecting deer to wander to our spring-fed pond for a cool drink may never leave my mind. The thought of going hunting with him struck fear deep in my heart – I wasn't certain that I could not *not* shoot him while out in the woods. That surely would have been easier than launching a bullet into the head of a beautiful innocent creature of Nature. I managed to always wiggle my way out of it – I was *sick* a lot.

When I was 13, my father spotted a BOY in the woods in our back yard where my sister and I were camping.

He fired *warning shots* with his rifle into the air (that's what he said, however, it sure looked like clumps of dirt and grass that were flying in the woods!). My boyfriend hopped on his bicycle and peddled out of there so fast that I think he left a smoke trail! He was an English exchange student (I think I was in love with his accent) and I was forbidden to see or speak to the English trash ever again, which was not difficult to obey -- it's not like my boyfriend was seeking to deepen our relationship! He never spoke to me again. Dad had names for every human *brand* but his own; his bigotry made me want to spit.

Another time when I relocated to Thomasville, Georgia with a boyfriend, I decided to leave him after too many weird cocaine adventures and one incident of physical abuse. A woman I was working with came to collect me and my things and he too pulled a gun on us. He said he was only shooting at the bushes but dirt and rocks were falling from the sky and landing all around us which only enriched the already adrenaline-filled moment. Somehow we got away uninjured.

And one last adventure that I'll mention…

When I was eighteen I went to New York for a commercial audition. Afterwards I went to a club with my fiancé (I had a few) and we were invited to an after-hours party with a couple we met at the bar. As it turned out, we were the party. He pulled a gun on us and wanted to "play". Dissociating and totally going into fight or flight response (not to mention all the alcohol blurring the event), I cannot remember to this day how we got out of there.

Drugs and alcohol can introduce one to some pretty sketchy characters and that can easily and quickly turn into a life-threatening nightmare. It's a wonder that I'm here today to tell about it.

Babies, Engagements and
Marriage, Oh My...

By the time I was twenty-two, I had been engaged to be married twice and was pregnant with my first child by her fifty-two year old father. Sure sounds like I came out of the pits of hell pretty much unscathed, doesn't it? I had a number of well-meaning people advise me on getting an abortion but I refused. I had a deep sense that this baby was going to be the answer to my searching.

As beautiful and amazing as she was (and still is), it turned out that she was not the answer either. She did however, give me a reason to live (something I desperately needed) and she gave me my first experience of unconditional love.

> *"If you cannot be at ease with yourself when alone, you will seek a relationship to cover up your unease. You can be sure that the unease will then reappear in some other form within the relationship, and you will probably hold your partner responsible for it."* ~ Eckhart Tolle

Unfortunately, by then I was drinking every day. I was in the throes of my own alcoholism (not knowing it of course – denial is such an amazing experience!) and was frantically searching for something to make my life complete or at least more comfortable. After a number of unhealthy relationships that revolved around alcohol and cocaine, I met the man who would become her legal father, help raise her and take care of me (little did either of us know that I was progressing well in the school of alcoholism and dysfunction was my major). I was twenty-five and my daughter was two when we married him; she was our flower girl.

Looking back at the wedding photos, it's hard to believe that I had actually pulled an all-nighter with the many gifts of cocaine that I received before our nuptials. My husband caught me on our wedding

60

night in the kitchen doing lines of cocaine while pretending to be studying for a college final exam. God, I could see the heartbreak in his eyes as he just stood there speechless. The weight of the guilt and shame I felt could have sunk a ship.

I had no idea why I couldn't just stop and go to bed – after all, it was our wedding night! That was the first time that I considered the possibility that I might have a problem.

The next day I called the 1-800-cocaine help-line and made an appointment with a counselor. He used a lot of scare tactics in hopes of shaking me up enough to quit all substances and get on with my life like a respectable young wife *should*. He obviously did not know much about addicts or alcoholics – most of them cannot be scared clean or sober.

Our life looked so perfect on the outside but on the inside I was dying. We had a beautiful home with an in-ground pool, and a thirty-four-foot sailboat out on the ocean. My husband made good money and knew how to handle it. One year later we had a beautiful son.

I was six-months pregnant when my corporate career ended as I got laid off. I took some time to be with our daughter and the baby to come while only working part time consulting. I did manage to keep the drinking limited to wine only while pregnant but was not able to give up the cigarettes.

Marriage and the proverbial white-picket-fence did not bring the peace and bliss I had imagined. I began in the mid-1980's with self-help workshops and retreats (LifeSpring training – basic, advanced, leadership, master and staffing) and many books. Acting classes and Community Theater also engulfed many hours of my time. I thought that if I could just have a little more fun in my life, things would feel better.

My son was born in April of 1986 and I went back to work in October of the same year. I had been in the restaurant/service industry off and on at least part time since my teens and I was good at it. I was looking forward to some time out of the house and to making some money of my own – especially since the allowance my husband was giving me was a pittance of what I was used to having in my pocket. However, food service and bartending is typically not a safe environment for someone with a drug and/or alcohol problem.

Coke – The Real Thing...

By 1989, cocaine (along with alcohol of course) was pretty much a daily fare. I had discovered how to embezzle money out of the company I was working for and was able to spend hundreds of dollars on cocaine and drink for free all night long while working. The coke kept me from crashing and the alcohol was my best friend. I had wonderful enablers around me at all times.

Strangely, my husband never interrogated me about my slipping into bed at four and five AM after work. I don't think he wanted to know. Or perhaps it was a passive-aggressive tactic to drive me crazy. It definitely fueled the fire of guilt for me and had my mind in a tazmanian-spin trying to figure out what he was thinking while I was lying there next to him cocaine-stimulated and whole body vibrating!
We had our first big vacation in March of 1989 and went to the British Virgin Islands. The flight there

was torture, as I was on the tail-end of a three-day coke-bender and could not get my hands on any more for the trip. Thank goodness the plane was not packed and I did get to stretch out for a few hours. Oh the agony of *crashing*! The plane going down would have been a welcomed relief. Words cannot describe the mental, emotional and physical pain of the kinds of hangovers I experienced. The nausea, the feeling of a bleeding, swollen and beaten brain, the shakes and the whole body exhaustion were just some of the physical fun of the event. The mental and emotional anguish fluctuated depending on the depths of my despair and confusion.

After the longest flight of my life, we arrived in Tortola, BVI. We chartered a fifty-foot sailboat with some friends of ours from church.

Oh god, how in the hell can I keep up this façade for ten whole days?

Fortunately, we did have quite a bit of alcohol on the

boat and every time we went to shore for anything, I always managed to belt down a few extras. The most wonderful sighting for me was a bar on the way to the ladies room that was out of view of the table we were sitting at – the bartender could never get that drink to me fast enough to soothe the swells of anxiety at the possibility of getting caught! I was also constantly on the lookout for someone who might be a good candidate to pop the cocaine question to.

My husband never really said much about my drinking. The greatest part of it was hidden from him and if he suspected that I was still using coke, he never mentioned it. Most of the time before going anywhere I would *pre-drink*, knowing that it would not look good if I drank as much as I wanted to. He would often just raise his eyebrows or ask me if I really thought another drink was a good idea as I was pouring the alcohol or ordering more than anyone else while we were out.

Often he was baffled by how tipsy or downright drunk

I could get on *just a couple of drinks*. If he had any idea how much I was really drinking, I'm sure he would have had more to say about it!

Sadly, the often dreamed of Virgin voyage in blue waters and cloudless skies, quickly turned into a heartbreaking journey when I came out of an alcohol black-out, crying and talking with my husband. It took a few minutes and some fancy-word-work to figure out what we were discussing and soon realized that I had asked him for a divorce. We still had seven days left to our vacation. Shit.

We survived the rest of the trip and once we got home, I stayed with a friend for a few weeks while trying to figure things out. My husband moved into the guest room for our in-house separation. We went right into couples counseling and divorced anyway a year later. He just couldn't fix me – nor did he try. It was me who wanted him to make me happy.

Fill me up for god's sake, can't you see I'm dying?!

Cracking Up...

Cocaine evolved into crack – I don't know how. I mean, I had seen stuff on TV where people were just sitting there, propped up against the wall in a stupor and looking like something from *The Return of the Zombies*, but I did it anyway. Actually, my coke-connection cooked up some cocaine for us one night (I had freebased once before in 1981) and I just thought we were smoking a more pure version of coke – you know, like all the crap was burned off. After that, she'd deliver bags of stuff that was more of a yellowish color and she always just called it *rocks*. We would smoke one bag after another and hours would turn into days. With each sunrise I always promised that this morning I am going home, right after we finish this one, I am definitely going home!

I despised the birds for singing to me "morning has broken" and I was still up. I ached deeply on the long rides home from the crack house and couldn't help but hate the *morning people* that I'd see out walking or jogging. With my bug-eyed look hidden behind dark shades and running on no sleep for days, every electron of my being would scream out to them as I passed them by, "How the hell do you do it?! Why can't I be more like you?!" The only time I could be considered a morning person were the many mornings that arrived without any sleep.

It didn't take long for crack to almost kill me. If the crack did not kill me, the secrets and lies would. My ex-husband and I had shared custody; he had the kids for a week and then I'd have them for a week. My week off would be a hazy chase of rocks, rocks and more rocks with plenty of alcohol in between. My week on would be a balancing act of taking care of my addictions while doing my best to take care of the kids, not get caught (by my children, neighbors or the police) and not kill myself!

The lifestyle was insanity-making and emotionally challenging to say the least! The anxiety that would torment me while waiting for the next delivery or trying to figure out a scheme so I could go 'pick up' had me exhibiting some pretty unbalanced emotions. I could easily *snap* over *nothing* and scream like a crazy woman at one or both of the kids – scaring them half to death I'm sure. I hated recognizing the fear in their eyes as that same fear I experienced as a little girl but couldn't stop myself.

I remember one scene when my daughter (probably around ten years old) was complaining about some discomfort in her life – shuttling between two homes as I recall – and I started yelling at her. I told her that she was spoiled and that she had no idea how good she had it! I wrapped up my rampage with 'at least she wasn't being beaten or sexually molested by anyone'! She calmly stated that pain was relative, that she had no idea what it was like to live in that environment but that on the scale of pain she had experienced in her life, this one was really bad.

Out of the mouths of babes.

70

I stood there dumbstruck and didn't say another word. She was absolutely right, pain is relative. I've never forgotten it.

I never set out to disappear into a stupor of drugs or alcohol. Most of the time, the story my mind would tell me was 'we will just have one or two this time and stop' and one or two always turned on the compulsion for more. And more was never enough.

I signed myself into a detox in 1992 with the goal of coming clean from crack. While there, I had to go to AA meetings and talk with a counselor. I could not believe what some of the people were saying about their lives and what alcohol had done to them. I thought 'my god, for sure if I ever get that bad, of course I will quit'! I could not imagine wetting myself, throwing up on myself, leaving my children, etc. The stories were hair-raising to me but I was not concerned because I was convinced that alcohol was not my problem.

Before I went into the detox, I called my "friends" and told them all that no matter what I say when I get out, do NOT give me any more crack. I drank the day I got home and within one week I was using crack again.

I went on an eight-day crack-bender in August of 1994 and had family and friends trying to find me (the kids were at summer camp). The man I was seeing (God, engaged again!) broke into my apartment with my ex-husband and searched the place for clues to my whereabouts. Like something out of Sherlock Holmes, using gravestone rubbing technique, my fiancé used the edge of the pencil lead and very gently shaded the paper to lift the number that had been written on the previous page of the pad, magically the number appeared. Once he had the phone number, he called on a friend at Ma-Bell to get the name and address – bingo, they found me and truly not a moment too soon.

I had just come out of what was later labeled as a *cocaine coma* – I just thought I was having a really cool out of body experience. My connection and her partner were freaking out when I wasn't responding to anything, but I felt fine. I was in the air watching the whole weird event – *me* just sitting there frozen in the chair with the crack pipe in my hand and the two of them yelling at me (and each other) trying to get me to snap out of it. I thought it was all a bit comical until I discovered that I was not sure I could get back into my body. I began feeling a bit panicked and eventually was thrown back into the human lump in the chair. How heavy. Anyway, my fiancé came barging in and carried me out like a baby – totally against my will because we hadn't finished smoking the resin yet and I did not want to leave that behind!

I managed to bounce back from that with the help of an eighteen-month out-patient program for crack/cocaine addicts. I walked into the program that my fiancé had so skillfully found for me – the only woman – and sat down with ten men who were trying to do the same thing as I was – live on this planet without a buffer.

I drove twenty-five miles four times a week for what seemed like forever and towards the end of my commitment to the program, only twice a week. I thought I must be amongst the very few women who suffered from crack addiction but I later found out that quite a few women had called inquiring about the program although they did not want to be the only female there. I would have stood on my head in a room with a hundred men if that's what it took to be released from the clutches of crack addiction. I just couldn't live like that anymore but was not able stop on my own. Women continued to call about the program and because there was now one female participant, me, I guess it wasn't quite as intimidating, so eventually a few other women joined our group.

I signed up for every extra study they presented, mostly for the money they offered (twenty-five to fifty dollars) and partly because I wanted to find out what the heck was wrong with me. They had studies for women suffering from PTSD, which I apparently had, and studies for addicts who had been abused as

74

children (that one seemed like a no-brainer to me) and other various studies that I *qualified* for. None of it seemed to change my perspective at all or make me better in any way but it helped their numbers and I got paid so everyone was satisfied.

The most important thing was that the ultimate goal was achieved – by November of 1994 I was finally able to put the crack-pipe down and keep it down. I guess I had finally had enough because one thing that I have learned in getting clean and sober is that you can't scare an alcoholic or an addict – they just have to be done and that only happens after experiencing every ounce of the agony that we are meant to experience, even if it takes us to the grave; which is where I thought it was taking me, and I was ready.

I began slipping [deeper] into the underworld during one of the last crack-benders that I went on just before quitting completely with the assistance of the program I was enrolled in. It was shortly after Halloween 1994 and on day three of this bender at the crack-house I was peering out the window (more like pacing and waiting for the next delivery to arrive) and was stunned to see such a gruesome Halloween exhibit. There was a picket fence around a small building and strewn on it were bleeding, deteriorating, convulsing and dying or dead bodies. I couldn't believe the town would allow such a hideous display and said so. My supplier looked out the window, said that there was nothing there (I thought she was kidding!) and then she 'shut me off' – fear I guess of the previous incident when I had left my body. That was not my only experience of the darker side but it was the first one that had a profound and lasting effect.

It was not easy sharing some of these most vulnerable and embarrassing moments with people – I had an image to keep up you know and I didn't want to be judged. I'm sure my fear of being judged was rooted in the fact that I was judging every one of the men in my group. My first week in the program when I had to share in the circle, I sat up straight, cleared my throat and said, "Well, I never got as bad as smoking *crack* but I did freebase coke quite a bit and purchased a lot of coke that was already cooked up for me." The laughter that created made me wish I could die right there in front of them all. Very gently, I was given the definition of crack: a chemically purified, very potent cocaine in pellet form, typically smoked in a glass pipe. Ahem...duh!

The group leader and the program psychiatrist hinted that I might want to attend a twelve-step program for support and perhaps quit drinking entirely but I'd been there already (maybe a handful of meetings) and thought that *those* people were really sick.

Check Out Time...

By 1997 I got to experience a lot of the things that I'd heard people talk about in the few meetings I had attended; regularly driving drunk or in blackouts, passing out in strange places, throwing up blood, wetting myself, peeing in public, sleeping with people I didn't want to be with, a night in jail, drinking all day and now to include mornings, weight gain, swollen liver, yellowish skin and eyes, gouty arthritis so bad that I was in a wheelchair for a week, dysfunctional thyroid, bleeding ulcer, depression, suicidal thoughts, and the list goes on. Clearly I was dying.

The insanity of it all had gone beyond unbearable and I couldn't understand why I was here or what the hell my purpose was. I very much wanted to be a good mother and on the outside it looked as though I wasn't doing too badly. On the inside I felt like a fake. I did all the things that a mother is *supposed* to do but so much of it was done with dread in my heart. I dreaded the parent-teacher meetings, knowing that I was going to have to be eye-to-eye with someone who probably had not had a drink that morning to talk about my children and their well-being.

Taking my daughter to dance class was another activity that caused a tight knot in my belly. I did not want to have to sit in the lobby and do the chit-chat thing with all the other mothers – talk of renovations, decorations, cookie recipes and proud parent *blatherings* would drive me out of my mind; I just couldn't get interested. I usually went for a drive (or sat in the parking lot) and drank. It was the same way for their sports activities; I wanted to want to be there but it seemed so insignificant. I always had a shot of something in my coffee-to-go mug to help ease the pain – the pain of not being who I thought I should be and also not knowing what that was. I did not feel equipped with the skills to do this 'life-thing'. There were many times that I thought I knew to the depths of my soul that the kids (and the planet) would be better off without me – I just didn't have the guts to end my miserable life.

I remember time and again near the end of my drinking when my daughter would return the *good-bye* note – mostly illegible – to me before her three years younger brother could see it. I don't recall writing any of them. What does come to mind is the desperate feeling of 'I'm dying' and the many times that I thought, 'okay, this is the night that I've gone too far and will not be waking up in the morning'. So in that state of mind, I guess I wanted to say goodbye to my children, apologize to them for dying and ooze with love for one last time. But then, morning would come and there I would be again, still stuck in a body that just would not let go.

I was on antidepressants for the last three years of drinking and that's when the thoughts of suicide became even more intolerable. I won't give a dissertation here about the destruction that most medication does to the body, mind and spirit, just know that I have one. It comes through personal experience and is backed with now years of research.

In June of 1997, in a blackout, I swallowed every prescription in the medicine cabinet (there were quite a few) and chased them down with a bottle of tequila – after drinking all day with a "friend". In the wee hours of the morning wearing only a tee shirt and my underwear, I dragged my blankie with me and curled up on the railroad tracks out in the woods to die. The train had not run on those tracks for years; just goes to show you how clear my thinking was that night.

For years I could not recall anything about that illustrious event but something began leaking into my consciousness over time and though it's not like a memory, more like a feeling, I know that I was on my knees crying out to a God that I felt had abandoned me and praying for help like I had never prayed before, desperately and from the depths of my soul.

My call must have been heard because someone dialed 911. To this day I don't know who or how anyone knew that I was there in the woods but someone did and it was not my time to check out. My guardian angel was taking care of me I suppose. I vaguely remember the paramedics reviving me and asking me a bunch of questions about what I had taken then I slipped back into the fog. I was rushed to the hospital, stomach pumped, spent two days in progressive care and then shipped off to the ward where they take all sharp objects and shoelaces away and there is only one handle on the door – on the *other* side. I was there for four days before I remember anything. I was upset with some people for not coming to see me sooner when actually they were the first ones there, but my brain was still 'on hold'. I spent five days there detoxing and even though I hated AA meetings and was forced to attend while in detox, I finally decided that I would check it out for a while and give that twelve-step program a shot (no pun intended).

As I was leaving, my doctor sat me down for an exit interview. He was going over a number of things and could see that I wasn't paying much attention as I had my eye on the door and was really just ready to go. That's when he grabbed my hand to get me to look at him – he had a very serious look on his face – while he went on to tell me that my incident was a very near death experience. He pointed to numbers and said that he had never seen anyone, especially a woman my size, with a blood alcohol count (BAC) of .368 (.50 being death) and that he wanted me to know how lucky I was to be alive.

I was not feeling very lucky nor was I very happy that I was still alive but I acknowledged his vital message.

I won't go on about all the many mishaps that happened in my drinking and drugging days but suffice it to say that there were MANY! I heard once in an AA meeting when I was trying to get sober in my early months, that when alcoholics hit bottom, they start digging. I didn't know what that meant at first. After hitting bottom a few more times and each one being worse than the last one, I finally understood the metaphor!

I started my journey in recovery in June of 1997 and was finally able to stop 'slipping and nipping' in December that year.

One would think that after such an event as my last big drinking excursion, that of course, of course I would stop drinking! Not so for an alcoholic. See I didn't know how bad I really had it – again, denial is a tricky bugger! During my drinking years I would try different things that I had heard from different folks in order to not cross over that line from happy-tipsy to annihilated or blacked out – things like:

- a glass of water in between drinks
- a big meal before going out
- milk in my drinks
- switching to alcohol that I don't like as much
- only beer
- only wine
- only mixed drinks and no shots

The problem with these solutions was that they always led me back to my drink of choice, always. Water in between drinks only made me pee more and by the time the buzz really got going, I'd wonder what I was so concerned about in the first place and skip the water for more booze. A big meal only made it messier later if I threw up. Milk in my drinks helped me to pack on some pounds and again, the buzz always led me back to my favorite cocktail – vodka, neat please (the identical drink that I had so harshly judged my mother about). The same with drinking alcohol that I didn't particularly like, or drinking only beer or wine, and not doing shots – it didn't matter what trick I tried, once the juice was in me, the gig was up, the chase was on, responsibilities took a back seat and my favorite bottle always showed up. Even when I really wanted to be reliable and show up for engagements, all it would take is the lying head to tell me that 'it'll be different this time and we'll stop in for just one'. One always led to one more, etc.

Help, I Need Somebody...

I had twelve consecutive years of therapy helping me to heal my childhood wounds and that only began to get very real for me when I got sober. I was in therapy with the same therapist for eight years before getting sober (the same woman my husband and I saw while trying to figure out our marriage). This again is another very good example of how good alcoholics are at hiding 'the other life'. I did lines in my therapist's bathroom. I came in for appointments doused in perfume and well-rinsed with mouthwash after drinking and using coke all night but I was *responsible* and most of the time, right on time – not very often did I cancel – and not very often did I go very deep.

After four years of sober therapy, it was a mutual decision to end my counseling. My therapist actually said I was *done* on a number of occasions two years prior but she was my security blanket at the time – I think having that outlet helped to keep me sober in the early days of giving it all up.

I was going to Alcoholics Anonymous practically every day, Incest Survivors Anonymous once or twice a week and an occasional Al-Anon meeting. I joined a twelve-week support and work-study group for abused women in my area which mostly focused on exercises out of a book called *The Courage to Heal*.

I had so much fear that it was oozing out all over my life. I just wasn't accustomed to doing anything without some sort of life-softener in me. For instance, I had no idea what to say to people after "Hi, how are you?" mostly because I detested chit-chat but partly because I had no social skills at all and so I'd duck and swerve to not bump into people I knew while out and about. Other times, it's like the whole world just all of a sudden became too big and overwhelming and I couldn't breathe. This wonderful experience could happen while out doing something as benign as grocery shopping. There were many times that I left my shopping cart full of groceries right there mid-panic attack and exited stage right as fast my little feet would carry me out of the store.

It wasn't fun trying to live life on life's terms, not to mention that at three months sober I gave up cigarettes too! I kept having the thought, 'what the hell do people do for fun if not drink – bowl?' God, no!

I had always had alcohol as my fall-back buddy and best friend for everything; it was always there for me. Drinking gave me the personality and courage to dance, date, have sex, talk to people, work, mother, tolerate chit-chat, well, you get the idea. If there wasn't going to be alcohol at the *function*, my attendance – if at all – was brief for sure! For the majority of my life, it had been the center of everything. It was really no wonder that I was so lost without it.

After giving up drugs and alcohol I discovered that I had what western medicine labeled as Obsessive Compulsive Disorder (OCD) and Attention Deficit

Disorder (ADD). I recall many times in early sobriety while out for a walk that all of a sudden I would realize I was counting my steps again – I'd be in the hundreds before I became consciously aware of it! Another fun OCD anomaly would be my mind clutching onto a few words in a song and repeating them over and over and over…something as pleasurable as "Little Willy, Willy won't go home but you can't push Willy round Willy won't go, try telling everybody but oh no, little Willy, Willy won't go home!" SECOND VERSE, SAME AS THE FIRST! Oh, you would not have survived in my head in those days.

In addition, the fear was so great that I occasionally could not leave the house to even take a walk around the block. My AA sponsor would come over and walk with me until my body could do it without an escort (she was more like a distraction for my distorted mind at the time).

And finally, another entertaining glitch about OCD, is

the dramatic events it would visualize. I could step into the bathroom after not being home for a bit and all of a sudden be struck with fear from just looking at the shower curtain because my mind would flash pictures of one or both of my children in there strangled and dead. Or, my daughter would be a few minutes late coming home, the phone would ring and in an instant I'd see a car crashed and rolled over the embankment and out of sight with her lying there, bleeding and dying. What's worse is I had a deep belief that what you fear you draw near and the more I tried to get rid of the image, the bigger and more detailed it became.

How I endured the insanity, I'll never know. Fortunately, many people do not have to dive this deeply into the *alcoholic crazies* before getting help.

> *"Just as the eagle uses the wind to take flight, take whatever is coming against you and use it to lift yourself higher."* ~ *Paramahansa Sri Nithyananda*

Thank God all of that healed over the first couple of years after getting sober. I don't know how people live with it. I imagine much longer

90

and I too would have been medicated – believe me, it was suggested. The ADD is still a part of my daily life but I have learned to relax and accept it while making adjustments when necessary rather than trying to *overcome it*. Actually, I think ADD is just the body's way of saying, "Presence please, one thing at a time."

My sponsor was also an incest survivor and she had just the things I needed to get me through the worst of my early sobriety anguish. I had twenty-seven years of feelings to feel and nothing to mask the misery. Thankfully, I had people to help me – I could not have done it alone. My sponsor told me to call anytime for anything and that's just what I did.

Without anything to soften the edges of reality, my world came crashing in. I had body-memories and flashbacks of my childhood that seemed so real I thought I was losing my mind. I would come out of an 'emotional blackout' and find myself in the basement, curled up in the corner and not knowing what had happened. Sometimes at hours as ludicrous as 3 AM, I would call her and she would bring me back into my body by doing some visualization with me, showing me how safe, protected and loved I am, then she would verbally coax me to the freezer and have me put an ice cube in my hand as we talked. That always landed me right back in my body but I could not think of it while in the throes of a crisis. She was a genius.

The white-hot rage that was emerging was another joy of sobriety. I had so much rage that at times I felt as if I could tear down city blocks with my bare hands. I got a clear understanding at that point how people could just *pop*, I felt close to it.

I didn't know that I'd been dissociating pretty much all of my life. What an amazing skill and to get so good at it that I couldn't even see it any longer was even more incredible to me. Whenever anything got uncomfortable for me, I'd just leave my body and go on autopilot. It was a wonderful help in my childhood for all the abuse but did not serve me well in my adult life!

I remember driving away from a therapy session and all of a sudden looking around in panic because I had no idea where I was! I called my therapist crying and described my surroundings and she guided me until I began recognizing the area. After that session, she started doing some serious grounding with me towards the end of our appointments.

A Change of Scenery...

All of my life, I thought that my relationship problems were directly related to the abuse from my father. I thought that I was damaged goods and could never have a long-lasting and meaningful relationship with a man. In the early 1990's I got my heart broken from a guy that I thought I really loved – we had been together for almost three years. He broke up with me when I signed myself in for my first detox for crack. He was blown away when I told him I was smoking crack and needed help – the dishonesty was too much for him and he left. That was when I decided that the reason I couldn't have a lasting relationship with a man was because I wasn't meant to be with men and began experimenting with women.

I had a number of wild experiences, many of them more than 'just the two of us'. When I got sober, I stopped dabbling in the masculine forms, went strictly women and came out as a lesbian. It was the second time that my therapist's straight-faced demeanor cracked; the first had been when I told her a story about cocaine. Incidentally, it is no wonder that so many alcoholics/addicts who die of health issues or suicide baffle the minds of many people around them; often they never suspected any trouble at all. Chameleons are good at adapting to their environment and hiding. My father had pretty much the entire outside world fooled! I sat in stunned amazement at his memorial service by all the beautiful things that many people were saying about the monster I grew up with. Didn't they *know* him?

Back to women…

I had a couple of relationships that only lasted a few months in my first year of sobriety. I then started seeing a woman who was just perfect for me – a therapist. We had a lot of fun together and she gently pointed when my perceptions were a bit skewed. I loved the warmth, safety and nurturance of a woman's arms and this woman was someone I thought I could spend the rest of my life with. After five months (and against her better judgment – I talked her into it) she moved in with me and my two children. Everyone liked her and again, my family was making adjustments to accept the new version of me. However, within about five or six months, I all too soon discovered that she was not the answer to the unending internal abyss that continued to swallow me up. I didn't know what was wrong with me! She was a wonderful person who loved me dearly and I was restless, unhappy and empty. I asked that she move out and we continued to be close friends until the threat of a man in my life became a real factor about six months later.

I silently slipped into a deep dark depression when she moved out towards the end of 1999. When she later cut all ties and I was pretty much ostracized by many in the gay community of our area, I felt so very lost and alone. By the end of my drinking, I had pretty much drank all of my friends out of my life. They had had enough of my dysfunctional behavior. Once getting sober and 'coming out', my new friends were

> *"It's exhilarating to be alive in a time of awakening consciousness; it can also be confusing, disorienting, and painful."*
> ~ Adrienne Cecile Rich

mostly gay and lesbian. So there I was, alone again and not fitting in. Ugh...it's how I spent most of my life. This world just did not seem to have a place for me. Even with my friends of the past, no one was allowed too close; safety in distance you know! I didn't know what was going on with me or how to fix it – I just wanted to feel okay here in this body – I thought something relatively close to normal would be nice!

That depression lasted five months. I did it without drugs, alcohol or pharmaceuticals. There were days that I would be in the fetal position in the corner of my bed with the covers over my head and not move all day. I did not want to live. I did not know how people did life here on this planet! What is it all about??

Slowly, off and on, the darkness would subside a bit. In those moments of freedom from the depths of hell, I began having memories of my childhood that I had

97

never considered before. Little ones. Things like, 'geez, Dad was so insecure and jealous – even of us kids – that Mom did not dare to comfort us'. And, 'the love from Mom was so constrained that it rarely felt genuine'. And, 'her fear of Dad's temper and jealousy was so great that she acted hateful to us just to keep peace with him'. From having those little memories, a major epiphany erupted – I am looking for a little girl's love and nurturance from her mother in intimate relationships with women – from that moment on, the sexual attraction was gone and soon after that the depression lifted too.

What a trip this life-thing is!

It is not easy being all over the place with beliefs and ways of being – and especially difficult when trying to make sense of it all while sharing life with my children. They sure saw a lot in their tenure with me. My son approached me with a raised eyebrow and a wise-little-smirk on his face one day soon after I came out as heterosexual again and said, "So let me get this straight – ahem, no pun intended – so first you were hetero, then you were bisexual, then you were lesbian and now you are straight again?" I didn't have anything to say but *yes*.

Let the Real Search Begin...

Once getting sober, I had nothing to ease that constant feeling of not belonging here. I just wanted to *want* to be here. It was as if I turned left when I should have gone right and landed on the wrong planet! I had no idea where my people were or who my leader was.

Sobriety is where my serious seeking began. It's not like I went looking for it initially; the Bible and a southern God had instilled enough fear, distaste and disbelief in me that I was finished with religion – not knowing at the time that a spiritual life did not have to be at all connected to religion, per se. A man from my 'crack program' suggested I read *The Celestine Prophecy* and once I finally did get around to it, the book blew me away. I read it again when I got sober and the next book that landed in my lap that had a profound effect on me was *Conversations With God*. I didn't know that we could have a God *like that*. From there, my perception of God began to expand and I devoured as many spiritual books and attended as many heart-opening or spiritual-type trainings and workshops as possible. Each one sparked a little more hope and shifted my perspective just a bit more than the last.

I have tried so many things over the years; Christianity (trying to reach the Christ), meditation groups (hosted and taught them), hundreds of books, Reiki journey started in 1998 (and still a wonderful blessing in my life), years of Self Realization Fellowship lessons with Paramahansa Yogananda, Keepers of the Flame with the Summit Lighthouse, Kriya Yoga and Kriya Theory classes with Swami Jayananda, Consciousness & Energy with Ramtha, Abraham Hicks, Gangaji, Deeksha with Amma and Bhagavan (twenty-one-day retreat in India March of 2006), hundreds of DVD's and audios from Deepak Chopra to Ekhart Tolle, and much more, none producing the lasting results I was looking for. It is not my intention to undermine the work of any of the above people or teachings because each one led me to the next page or chapter in my life.

101

Everything I have done, read and lived has brought me to deeper awarenesses.

Even the perpetual abuse I endured in my childhood has its place in my life now. If someone had tried to convince me of that possibility before I had some sobriety, recovery and healing in my life, I probably would have flattened them, perhaps not with my fists but certainly with my retaliatory tongue. I did not have a survivor's view of my desperate history – I was a victim and that was that! I was angry, sad, hurt and totally screwed up because of it and I looked for validation and sympathy when I spoke about it. To me, the thought of forgiving that evil creature of my past meant that what he did was okay – 'we'll just let bygones be bygones, okay?' That was not happening! Through therapy, meetings, talking with my sponsor, journaling and just sitting quietly with myself, eventually I began to see that he was still affecting my life, even though he'd been dead for years.

I pondered the possibility of forgiving him, not for him

but for me, so I could get on with my life and hopefully live a little happier. That form of forgiving released me from a victims perspective and opened me to a survivor's view, which was a profound event in my life. I had no idea that it was me, my attachments to the past, and all my beliefs that were keeping me stuck and in the grips of suffering. Over time, forgiveness quite slowly grew into compassion for a couple of very sick people, my dad and me. My view of him as a disgusting monster and a despicable human being was gradually shifting to seeing him as a person who had a mental illness and who was also suffering the pangs of his own past. At this point I noticed we were both changing and he had been dead for almost twenty years.

I do recall an incident prior to all of this where I had my first experience of compassion towards my father. When I was eighteen and waiting for an apartment to be available while the one I was moving out of no longer was, I landed back at Mom and Dad's house for a few months. It was very soon after my arrival that a cousin passed away in a car accident and my mother went to Florida to be with her sister and help her through the crisis of a lifetime, losing a child. While back on the home-front, old fear was a-brewing and I did not like being home alone with *him*, although at this point it had been four years since he had touched me.

One night soon after Mom had left, I was drifting off to sleep when Dad entered my room – old panic struck my whole being but then I noticed something different about him. He looked scared. With little boy fear, he asked if he could sleep with me and said that he was afraid of the snakes under his bed. Something different moved through my body and I was able to rise out of bed, take him by the arm and lead him back to his room. Using the flashlight I showed him that there were no snakes under his bed. He then said that they must have moved into his closet, so we opened that door illuminating all floor space and revealing no snakes. At that point he was able to go back to bed (alone!) and so was I. I laid there feeling so sad that he was so sick. I did not know at the time that his deterioration was the progression of alcoholism that I was witnessing (he had also shown signs of schizophrenia for as far back as I can now remember).

Getting back to what I was talking about in regard to forgiving; sometime soon after the forgiving began, I came to a place of acceptance. I was not trying to accept, it was just the outcome of forgiving. Forgiveness took a

> *"Forgiveness is the fragrance the violet sheds on the heel that has crushed it"*
> *~ Mark Twain*

long time and many prayers for it to begin to take shape in my life. At first I would pray for the willingness to forgive him because I still felt like I would somehow be letting him off the hook. But, eventually, the forgiveness began to permeate my heart and then acceptance of 'what was' opened me to a deeper level of healing and a richer perspective. This particular man was in my life as my father to do what he did for a reason; why, I do not know but I gained a deep sense of knowing that it was all part of a greater plan – one just out of my human reach.

As a young child, I had a fine-tuned, well-developed radar that knew when my father was getting out of bed and heading my way; I could feel it. As much as that stirs something deep in my belly just by writing it, I do know that it was the catalyst for my amazing sensitivity in the work I do and also just in being around people in general as an adult today. All I ever really wanted was to be happy but if that wasn't possible, the second wish was for all the pain to not be in vain.

Within a year of getting sober, Reiki found me. I had never even heard the word before. I first became interested in learning more about Reiki when a friend gave me a treatment before surgery and again immediately after the procedure. I was skeptical and thought that the heat I was feeling from her hands was some kind of trick. The results, however, made me an avid believer in the powers of this amazing healing energy. After the procedure, I felt great and had no need for pain medication. The healing was very quick and the scar is so small, it can barely be seen. The real surprise came later after a few more treatments when I no longer needed medication for my dysfunctional thyroid.

I couldn't wait to discover more about Reiki. I grabbed the first book I could get my hands on and then searched my area until I found a class; within twenty-four hours of making the initial contact with a Reiki Master I was in a Reiki level one class. Wow, what an experience. After the attunements (energy initiation) and while practicing hands-on, I could feel energy tingling in my hands, intense heat in my heart and it felt like my feet were barely touching the floor. At that moment, I finally knew what I wanted to be when I grew up! I couldn't wait for my Reiki level two class and then to start my master training. I have trained in many healing modalities since then and share them all with my clients to tailor-fit their needs but my first love is always Reiki, which is where my deepest healing took place.

Since then, I've experienced so much healing on many

levels that it would take a book to cover all the details. I'm sure that the Reiki assisted with all the epiphanies and emotional healing that I had around my mother and father stuff. That is how Reiki works. The energy goes where it is needed, (so simple!) at the best possible time and clears the underlying cause that is generating disease in the body/mind/spirit. It has been an amazing gift in my life and to be able to share that with others and see them heal on levels that they did not even know was possible really feeds my spirit.

The sensitivity I have when working with people is nothing less than miraculous. I can feel their discomfort either in my body or through my hands, whether it be physical or emotional and my hands know right where to go. This, I believe is a direct result of the years of abuse I was subjected to as a young girl. I recall, while lying in bed at night, every cell of my body would be standing at attention and on red alert, tuned in to any signs of movement from my father's end of the house. This exercise trained me to be intuitive at a level that I do not think would have been possible otherwise.

Getting a Life...

I liken getting sober to never coming out of amnesia and having to build a whole new life. For me there was nothing to go back to. For twenty-seven years I drank and used drugs and when I surrendered (or it surrendered me), I found myself in a very lost state. Alcohol took the edge off and softened my world just enough to help me do all those things in life that other people seemed to be equipped with the ability to do without it.

I didn't know how to communicate with my children without yelling at them when I was upset. I didn't know when I should say yes or when I should say no. I didn't know how to have boundaries or how to walk through fear. I didn't know how to agree to disagree with anyone. I didn't know how to be with feelings. I didn't know how to socialize with people. Everything in my life was done in an altered state so when the alcohol was gone, I had no idea how to live life on life's terms.

Slowly and over time as my sponsor worked with me, I began to get my land legs. I started applying her suggestions or comments that I heard in AA to my personal situations. I discovered that taking a brisk

> *As we express our gratitude, we must never forget that the highest appreciation is not to utter words, but to live by them. ~ John Fitzgerald Kennedy*

walk down the street and back could give me the distance I needed for clarity to arise before responding or reacting to one of my children's incessant requests. Meditation began to bring me peace that was spilling over into all areas of my life. Journaling was helping me to heal on many levels and was an amazing way to vent my unedited pain without hurting anyone. Addressing my fear of conflict by speaking up when it felt right for me to do so (and seeing that no one's head blew up) built confidence with each tiny step and made it easier for the next time. Practicing saying no helped me to be able to say it when it was needed. Setting limits and healthy boundaries came over time as I learned through experience, one person at a time, and through discussions with my therapist and sponsor. Reciting the serenity prayer many times during the day was very helpful: "God grant me the serenity to accept the things I cannot change; courage to change the things I can; and wisdom to know the difference." Remembering slogans in AA and applying them daily, as needed, helped when I was feeling overwhelmed: "This too shall pass", "One day at a time", "Easy does it", "Keep it simple" and many others.

It wasn't easy arriving here on this planet at thirty-seven years of age, ill-equipped to do life, looking like a grown-up and feeling like a child, while having two children to take care of and many other responsibilities. I just kept putting one foot in front of the other, going to AA meetings and asking for help. Before I knew it, sober-time was beginning to accumulate and I was starting to feel better, conduct myself better, think better and look better.

I recall hearing in early sobriety to 'keep the focus on yourself' and you will be surprised as you grow and change to discover how many people around you begin to change. I did not understand that at all but in time I was able to experience what it meant. The first ones I noticed the change in were my children. I was amazed to see how differently they were acting as they absorbed and responded to the changes in me; my perspective, my delivery, my level of patience, etc. I then began to notice the change in other family members, especially my mother with whom I had a strained and rather fragile relationship; we have a wonderful connection now. Gandhi said, "Be the change you want to see in the world." I get it.

Even though life was still throwing curve balls and forcing me to grow, I also began to notice some of the more pleasant things that were happening. The relationship with my children started getting better very soon after *I* started getting better. They were bringing friends home for dinner and for "family night". We would have a meal together and then play

113

games; Charades, Taboo, Cranium and many others. I never would have believed that it was possible to have so much fun without an alcohol stimulant. I cherished those moments with my children. I had missed so many sweet moments when they were younger; not so much because I wasn't there physically but because I was not entirely present; a part of my mind was always focused on sketching out my next opportunity to drink.

More and more my mind continued to clear, my health kept getting better and better and the relation to my past began to heal in stages that my body and heart could withstand.

Life began to look like something I might be interested in.

Blissings Please...

I've had many spiritual experiences in my life; I
dabbled in stuff as a kid but had some amazing things
happen as an adult...mind you, these all began
happening after I got sober. The AA sponsor I was
working with encouraged me to pray on my knees
until I could do it because I wanted to. The first few
times I got on my knees, before my lips began to
move, my silent prayer was 'oh god, I hope no one
sees me' and that was in the privacy of my own
bedroom. She also suggested books that would help
me to find a Higher Connection. I was so broken and
spiritually bankrupt when I began working with her
that I would have done just about anything she said.
Big things began to happen rather quickly as I was
humbled in many ways and as I stayed sober. The
following are just a few:

- Contact with an angel – who truly helped save my life in early sobriety and continues to pop in from time to time
- One (healthy) out of body experience
- I heard celestial music on a few occasions. The first time was a real kick! I was recuperating from some traumatic emotional healing and was meditating. All of a sudden, the most beautiful, full, rich extraordinary music like I had never heard before was filling all space – I could not tell where it was coming from! I opened the door and looked outside, not there, I went to the other side of the house and opened the window, not there. It did not seem to be coming from anywhere but *was* everywhere. My daughter looked at me perplexed and I asked if she could here *it*, she had no idea what I was talking about. Whew, good thing I know I'm not crazy (I think).
- While giving a Reiki treatment, I shifted into a 'different realm' and I felt like the person I was working on and I were one, everything was

One, but somehow *we* were soaring through space and everything was happening NOW – blissful eternity is the best way I can describe it. I started to look around as we were flying through space and suddenly realized that we were not flying through space, we WERE space, which surprised me, then cognitive brain kicked in and I crashed back in my body. It felt like I had been gone forever but only a couple of minutes had passed.

- I was in great emotional pain facedown on my bed and praying for answers when all of a sudden I saw infinite universes and galaxies before my eyes right there in my comforter – it was like peering through a portal – and I knew all the answers to Life – it felt like my heart was going to explode I had such joy and couldn't wait to write it down and tell everyone who would listen – it was gone in a flash, as fast as it came. I could not recall any of the details. Although, it was comforting (no pun intended) to have had the experience and to know that All Is Well.

- Just under two years (2001 – 2003), I was in an almost constant state of bliss where I felt love for all and everything. It wasn't like I was walking around in complete joy all of the time but no matter what happened on the outside, the peace I felt on my inside world was unshaken – like a warm current running beneath it all and even the *bad* felt *good*. That slowly faded into contentment and then into complacency followed by severe depression starting in January 2005 that lasted for two and a half years.

- I visited Ashland, Oregon (in answer to my heart's calling) for a thirty day visit January 2006 to find my spiritual connection and re-ground with Mother Earth and hopefully push through the other side of the horrific depression. I was led by a friend to a deeksha event, received the energy transmission and was put in an altered state for four days. One of the experiences during those four days happened while I was driving. A flock of birds flew overhead and all of a sudden I expanded into the ALL; I was everything, the birds, the vehicle, the trees, mountains, traffic…it was most amazing and I had tears of joy streaming down my face. Others like that one came and went over the four day period and then IT was gone.

- In the early months of the relationship with my partner, we were on the beach in Florida and in a flash, I experienced TRUE Love. We were just sitting there talking and all of a sudden, he was God Himself – the most beautiful and perfect being I had ever seen. My heart was so full of Love and intense heat that it felt as if it might burst – then poof, *we* were back, human to human, sand in our eyes and grit in our sandwiches.

The depression finally began to lift within about five months after my partner and I moved to Oregon, leaving behind his and my grown children and three young grandchildren.

The Void...

The two and a half years of depression was like something out of a fiction story – I didn't believe it possible to continue to breathe in and out in such a state. If I could have just figured out how to stop the breathing in and out, I would have. I am sure the earlier five-month depression tempered me somewhat to survive the two and a half year abysmal *life* but all I wanted was out. At this point, I suspected that most likely I would not kill myself but the thoughts of drifting away in a permanent sleep were enticing. I just didn't know how to do it. I pondered studying some Hindu Indian techniques where many yogis had consciously left their bodies and moved on to the next life but I figured I would probably never attain that ability since my agenda was 'suicide without pain or mistakes'. Somehow, at a deep level, I knew that I was not done here. So I searched and begged and prayed while trying every healing modality I could think of to fix the depression: diet shift, thought shift, exercise, yoga, all to no long-lasting benefit.

I did get some relief while working with clients. Helping them to feel better helped me for the time that I was with them. Once the treatment was over, so was my reprieve from the depression.

Waking up in the morning was like the movie *Ground Hog Day*, nothing had changed. There *it* still was, the hole in my soul and at this point I had nothing left to fill it with; I had used up everything. I pondered the movie and wondered if throwing myself in front of a moving vehicle or off a cliff would land me back in bed to the alarm clock going off and the life-sucking void that I continued to experience. Getting out of bed and starting my day was like dragging a carload of

> *"Through allowing, you become what you are; vast, spacious. You become whole. You are not a fragment anymore, which is how the ego perceives itself. Your true nature emerges, which is one with the nature of God." ~ Eckhart Tolle*

screaming two-year-olds to the dentist, it was a nightmare.

I have heard again and again that we teach what we most need to learn and I have repeatedly experienced that to be true. For years I have been sharing with clients how to drop into their feelings as they arise and encouraging everyone to fully experience them. In doing so, the energy passes through much more quickly. Feelings are like a young child constantly pulling at you until you give them the attention they are seeking. In many cases the root feelings originate from the past and are just frozen energy in the psyche waiting to be acknowledged. Once we allow it to be there, are fully alive and wholly present for it, we may see the connection to the past which will help to alleviate its power, but most importantly, the feeling gets full expression and often dissolves very quickly.

I was talking with a woman after an AA meeting and telling her about the brutal depression that was lingering in my life. She gave a comforting smile and gently asked, "Have you considered just allowing yourself to feel depressed? Or if you can, even thanking the depression for its presence in your life?"

Whoa, that sounded familiar! The first time I heard it was in the first few months of sobriety when my sponsor would tell me that I had plenty to be depressed, angry, sad, etc. about and would then tell me to feel it, to just lie down and cry or pile up some pillows and beat on them with my fists or a tennis racquet; hang up and thrash a punching bag; primal scream into a pillow or go for a drive to a secluded area with the windows up and scream deeply; whatever it took to feel what I was feeling as long as it didn't hurt me or another. I used all of the techniques and they all helped. I wondered how she knew these things. These simple techniques have assisted me and many of my clients and friends for years now.

HOWEVER, applying the technique of feeling the depression to the kind of depression that I was experiencing now was terrifying! I was having a hard

124

enough time semi-functioning in my life at the level of depression that I was already at! If I stopped trying to heal it, just let it *be*, or fully felt it, it might get worse and I couldn't BEAR that. Slowly, quietly in my mind (which was safer than my body) I began to say thank you to the universe for the gift of depression – not believing it at all but it was a start. When I did not dissolve into a smoldering pool of thick goo, I decided to *allow* myself to *feel* depressed for brief periods of time and discovered that feeling depressed sure did use less energy than trying to fix it. It really didn't take very long after that for the depression to begin lifting – wow.

Because of this little lesson, I am now much more alert and present for what is coming out of my mouth as I am sharing guidance with others. Often I notice a gem in the suggestions for me, too!

Life is Like a Box of Chocolates...

So, again I ask, what's it all about? Huh? Who am I
or rather what am I? Just when I think I've got things
figured out, IT changes. I've gotten to where I'm just
open to whatever the next turn in Life is for me
because I never know what I am going to get.

I have gone from guilt over my past to appreciation of
the lessons or seeds for growth.
I have never set out to
intentionally hurt anyone but I
did cause a lot of pain and
worry in the lives of many
family members, friends and
significant others. Though

> *A man of genius
> makes no
> mistakes. His
> errors are
> volitional and are
> the portals of
> discovery.*
> *~ James Joyce,
> Ulysses*

knowing on a deep level that it was all part of *our*
journey together for what we came to accomplish, I
can't help (yet) but feel some regret for the discomfort
that my *being* caused in people's lives, especially my
children's. Perhaps someday I'll be able to see how

126

important those *mistakes* were and gain a whole new appreciation of them but in the meantime, I do feel regret that I had to be the purveyor of pain for whatever the event was that needed to be played out. Life's journey is not always clear or comfortable.

I used to see those *woo-woo* people back in my less conscious days and thought that they were very strange. Today I am one of those woo-woos. Being a holistic practitioner, I cannot help but be of service now – it is part of me. I have given Reiki treatments on the beach – right out in public – and that never would have happened in my *other life,* I was just too self-conscious. Now, if a person is open to receiving and in need of an energy adjustment in some way, I help by sharing my experience and the energy of Love. Perhaps in some way that is fulfilling the childhood dream of being a doctor, except today, I assist people in healing rather than masking symptoms and cutting out body parts (I know there are a few doctors out there who are interested in Healing but the majority are not trained in that).

Did you know that there is only a two and a half hour *nutrition* requirement for all the years of study to become an M.D.? I was shocked when I discovered that. Food is the biggest contributor to the health of the body! Two and a half years of study would give a good deep appreciation of the importance of what we put in (and on!) our bodies and how deeply that affects

> *I have yet to meet a single person from our culture, no matter what his or her educational background, IQ, and specific training, who had powerful transpersonal experiences and continues to subscribe to the materialistic monism of Western science.*
> *~ Albert Einstein*

us, even two and a half months would give enough of a taste of the lies that we've been fed about food to trigger interest in more research, but two and a half hours!? From my perspective, it is no wonder so many are sick and dying, they just don't know. I do not judge ignorance because I certainly had no idea what processed, chemicalized, dyed, zapped and lifeless "food" was doing to me and my children until attending my first nutrition class. During week two, I came home from class dazed, opened the cupboards, started reading labels, about fainted, then filled four grocery bags with the poisonous items – I have not looked back since.

I have shifted from a self-employed computer consultant, drug-using, active alcoholic, cigarette smoking, coffee swilling, sugar binging, meat-eating, processed-food consuming, very unhealthy person to a clean and sober, nonsmoker, herbal tea drinking, sugar-free, chemical-free, healthy, organic vegan, Reiki Master, massage therapist, nutritional guide, and *spiritual* person who teaches others how to embrace a healthier lifestyle.

I'm also a sungazer who greets the sun with the birds and love in her heart! Who knew? Those days of aching as the sun was coming up because I had not yet slept have completely transformed.

Do not misunderstand, I am not saying that any of the above ways of being are *right* or *wrong*, I am just saying that it feels a bit more comfortable to be here in a healthier body with a more sane and balanced state of mind. We all need to do what we are doing until we cannot do it any longer – then the shifts take place – all in perfect divine timing. The strangest part of it all is that NONE of it was my idea. I did not consciously choose to be any of it. My life evolved organically without me having to *do* anything but be here.

And here I am, wondering what to write on the next page; still with that deep longing/ache that I can't seem to pacify with any of the sane and healthy practices of my new life.

As I've already mentioned, life off and on had been pretty surreal before getting sober, and it continues to be so now but in a different way. As I look around at the world, I think to myself that this has to be a dream (or an illusion) because it is too weird to be real. There are contradictions everywhere I look and so many perspectives that people have (and in some cases will kill for), that it just has to be an illusion – how can reality house so much *untruth*? How can billions of people, day in and day out go through their day just like they did the last one without questioning the insanity of the way that we are all living? Granted, some people are scratching their heads and saying, 'wait a minute, what's wrong with this picture' and some people are actually getting involved to make some changes but for the most part, people are sleep walking.

I know I'm digressing here but I feel this view needs to be expressed.

People have been anesthetized through media, television, religion, spiritual paths, drugs, chemicals, processed food and the material world and they do not even know it. I know because I was one of those people and somehow managed to escape years ago.

I was having a conversation with someone who, upon my recommendation, had viewed the movie *Zeitgeist*. He ardently disagreed with the importance of getting that information out to the masses – dissolving the myth of Jesus and other masters. He has a deep abidance in the value of myth and its role in the human psyche. I just stood there not really knowing how to respond. I thought, okay, a relatively harmless fairy-tale to share with a young child to inspire growth, vision and laughter is one thing, but to build empires on a lie or at least an exaggeration about "God's Son" and the many other messiahs is another. Shouldn't a myth be exposed as such? We are not little kids here waiting for Santa Clause or the Tooth Fairy.

Everyone is entitled to their perspective of course but millions and millions of people have been slaughtered or have given their lives (for god's sake!) to be right about their particular version of the story. Doesn't the danger and horror of that *way* outweigh the value of having something to hang my spiritual hat on?

This to me is too weird for words. How in the world has it gone on for this long? Wouldn't it be better for the whole world to know the truth so we can stop hating and killing each other in support of a partial

132

truth or a lie? For me, the research and information speaks for itself – watch the movie, and do some research.

I find great solace in knowing that we all live under the same holy, blessed, sacred, healing light and unconditionally loving *sun*, of God (or Creator) who shines equally on us all. The rest is a myth originated from the days of Egypt – an analogous story of movement through eras in the zodiac.

Please don't come with your torches and pitchforks, I am not saying that there wasn't a wonderful person named Jeshua Ben Joseph of Nazareth who shared with many people great love, healing, initiations, and some beautiful pointers to the Heart, but the rest of the story was potentially created to control us.

That'll shake some trees, I know.

As The World Turns...

Once sobriety was well established, the calling of the heart began to stir again. For ten full years in my sober life, I searched and explored the meaning of existence and wandered down many different paths of awakening. I was ready to give up, to stop all my practices, perhaps have a book-burning party, and maybe use all the CD's and DVD's as Frisbees. The effort of seeking was exhausting and I was running out of paths and energy. Although, I still could not deny the powerful tug at my heart for *something more*!

I have been told many times to be careful what I ask for – I just might get it. For a very long time, I have been calling for divine intervention in whatever way it has to come to assist me in shifting to a higher perspective; an awakening for life. As I mentioned earlier, I have had many mini-awakenings but nothing ever sustainable. I would be in an altered state for minutes, hours or days but it would not stick and I always returned to the status quo me. Ugh.

Still chasing that illusive carrot of enlightenment, early in 2007, I ventured into a meeting of another 'spiritual group' that met twice a month. However, as I sat there I had all kinds of judgments about how the meeting was run and about the teacher who was on speaker phone; it wasn't professional enough, or organized enough, etc., so I didn't think it was for me. It was their first meeting in the area and the last one that I attended for a while. Some months later something began whispering to my heart and I had to go again to see what the calling was about. It was an entirely different event for me; I guess I was *ready*. There was a visiting teacher facilitating and his words made sense to me. Rather than waking up, he was speaking of *Waking Down in Mutuality*. He was saying that he was aware of Consciousness *in* his body while at the same time experiencing an expanded state of Awareness. I hung on his every word as I had not heard any teacher or path speak of *including* the body in their awakening – not in this way, at least.

I was touched that evening by the honesty of the people who shared and I was moved to tears identifying with the pain that was expressed, the longing for something more, something else; for me it was a silent screaming heart. I did not speak that night but they certainly had my attention and I went back to the next meeting two weeks later. There was another teacher in attendance and after she spoke, she looked right into my soul (I felt) and to the best of my recollection said, 'and what about you, do you have something you would like to say?' Crack! That was the sound my heart made. Something cracked and it all came pouring out. I don't recall what all I said but I was crying and drooling and blowing bubbles and I did not care – someone just kept handing me tissues.

The most beautiful part of the experience was the feeling of being held while I unraveled, not in a physical sense but energetically so to speak. There was a feeling of such presence and attentiveness that it was palpable. As I finished the story of my 'aching and longing heart' the people there began to give feedback and I was again moved to my core with their words of support, compassion, identification and honoring. I remember thinking, 'wow, you mean you understand!? And it's really okay to feel all these things?'; there was a great sense of relief that ran through my body.

For my whole life, I had great difficulty *being* here. The world did not make any sense at all and I could not seem to find my purpose or place on this planet. I was certain that something had gone terribly wrong somewhere and I just landed on the wrong planet; lost on this desert island, completely misunderstood by the world and with such a longing to be home; an ache in my heart that couldn't be satiated with anything.

Things began to really stir once getting involved with *Waking Down in Mutuality*. That longing inside turned at times into cyclones of energy that made me

137

feel as if I would spontaneously combust if I did not find a release valve. Looking around at my life, it all seemed so meaningless and I really wished that I could find a way to the exit. That 'back-door' was like the contingency plan; I always took a bit of comfort in knowing that if life got any worse, (this longing, desperation, emptiness), ending my life was always an option.

At one point, someone handed me *Waking Down: Beyond Hypermasculine Dharmas"* by Saniel Bonder. I flinched and wanted to drop it and run. As the knot in my belly got tighter, something from within made me reach out and let it land in my hand. Even though I was breaking a promise to myself (no more books, paths, teachers or gurus!), I dove in and began reading that book and many others, attending workshops and going to all the meetings. In January of 2008, my partner and I even began hosting the meetings in our home because our prior host moved to California.

I read and re-read things; they spoke to my heart and I knew on a deep level that I was finally onto something, something Big. I took some words from one of the books I was reading, *White Hot Yoga of the Heart* also by Saniel, and turned them around a bit to make them into a prayer or an invocation, stating: "I pray for, intend, even insist upon whatever is necessary for my realization of Being to come to fruition as directly and rapidly as possible". Again, I will warn here to be careful what you ask for. Words this powerful, spoken from the heart can really turn up the volume on life! And it did! Very soon after that my whole world began to change.

Falling In ~ The Journey Home...

The first big occurrence: In January of 2008 I awoke to a voice that softly said, "It's time to write." My partner was away and I can tell you, that pretty much freaked me out. By the third morning the voice was so loud that I jumped out of bed, went to the computer and the words of this book began pouring through me. It came through in two parts. More about that later.

The second major happening: I had a kundalini awakening three months later in April. With that came such a feeling of purification, lightness. So much burned off. It was incredibly intense and not something that I would recommend to anyone given a choice! For me it was like a white-hot train ripping through the center of my body.

All this was occurring right around the time that my partner of four and a half years started backing away from our relationship. He began house-sitting (we had been having some relationship issues) and he was gone for weeks at a time. I kept falling deeper and deeper into every feeling, every experience, and I slowly came to realize that something very profound had shifted. I was no longer in the same relation to pain as I had been for so many years.

My eighteen year old cat, Tigger, passed on June 30th, my partner ended our relationship July 2nd, and that evening I was bit on my right leg by a brown recluse spider which caused great physical pain and fear as I watched the skin continue to deteriorate as if acid had been poured on it; it took a couple of months to heal and left quite a scar as a reminder of my initiation.

As I began to experience the losses, the first thing that happened was the heartache, great sorrow, deep misery that felt like it might be endless. Mentally I kept making my list over and over of all the things that I had to feel pain-filled about, which had been my modus operandi for most of my life. What was different with this grief was that I was not fighting any

141

of it. I was just falling right down into the middle of it, feeling it deeply, fully, expressing and venting it by crying, primal screaming, or punching pillows; whatever was needed in the moment to allow the feelings to fly freely. I kept "greenlighting" everything, allowing and welcoming it all, even my judgments about not being able to accept *whatever* in a particular moment. I was speaking openly, passionately and vulnerably to my newfound waking-down-family about my feelings. At times, the bottom of the emotion would seem to *drop out* and I would either land in a pool of peace or bliss. I remember thinking 'wow, you mean pain can be blissful or peaceful too'? Not resisting anything, everything began to change.

The double-whammy of losing Tigger and not having him as some comfort for the loss of my partner, our house, the recently built cottage for my clients and our garden, and also of losing my partner and not having him to console me for the loss of Tigger created a volcano inside of me that felt like it imploded once the eruption subsided and I landed right smack-dab in the middle of me; someplace I'd never been before…home…complete…nothing needed. All of a sudden, it all felt sacred, all of it, from the very

> *We shall not cease from exploration. And the end of all our exploring will be to arrive where we started and know the place for the first time.*
> *~ T. S. Eliot*

beginning of my life, every piece a gift to help me land here…Here. As I cried, now from a love that was alive in me, I wanted to thank my partner and Tigger for the gift they gave me. This heart that I thought was shattered and taking on one more battle-scar was washed clean and filled with amazing gratitude for Life and all its dips and curves. Love like no other…

Another thing that I noticed as I was spinning from the one-two punch was that there were no thoughts of suicide. I kept looking over my shoulder wondering 'hey, where's my back door?' – no back-up plan at all – just here.

What an incredible sense of freedom living in this
Heart space. How did I miss this all these years? So
close, so far, so beautiful, so very sacred.

Ode to Tigger

My Best Friend and his Sister chose me
Through my own two children,
Brother and sister
How did they know to arrive at the shelter
Fifteen minutes before we wandered in
Looking for a kitten –
The fulfilling of a Christmas promise

My children's insistence
On this two-year-old duo was unfaltering
Oh the heaviness when I, as a single mom,
Realized the 'new-cat-smell' would soon wane
My mind darted at ways to postpone the promise
Wondering why-oh-why wasn't there one
Fuzzy little kitten there to catch their hearts

Sooner than I would have guessed

I became caretaker of four

Two children, two cats and too much to do

For quality time with any of them

They saw me through my worst years

And were the brunt of my anger at times

They saw me finally hit bottom

And get sober in 1997, all of them

One by one

Leaving the nest

First my daughter

And then my son

They were the catalyst of a painful spiraling

Into myself

Who am I, if not Mom

Looking around every corner to find myself

I found two beautiful cats

They were there all along

Waiting patiently

For their turn

With my heart

Growing closer and falling
Deeper into Love with them
I began to discover
I am only the caretaker
Their job as One is so much greater
Healer, bringer of Peace, Love, Comfort,
Laughter and Joy

Confidant, companion, teacher
Dancer, guardian and seer
Love-bites, wrestler,
Stupid human tricks and purrs
Brilliant, tolerant,
Graceful, majestic
And loyal –
Yes loyal

I honor you Tigger
For your courage
And strength

To be all these things

And more

We've traveled together before,

My Friend

As you leave the nest

But not my Heart

And shed the physical body

Melding yet again into the One

Fly free,

Fly home

And keep me in your Heart for a while.

Before the turmoil and grief began, I had planned a trip to New York for a six-week Shamanic/Herbal Apprenticeship and then to move on to the Boston area for two weeks of work and a family visit. I ended up staying only one week in New York before moving on to Boston. I recall a sense of wondering why I was there, as the seeker that had been so much a part of my being seemed to have vanished. During the apprenticeship, I had many lessons in such a short period of time, mostly to listen to the inner guidance, always so wise. This trip so soon after my awakening was like the grounding of my transformation or cementing Being into this human form.

The following are some of the details of my experience, my reactions to them and how I felt supported by the universe through the whole process.

To begin with, nothing looked at all like what was advertised on the website for the apprenticeship. The workload was unfathomable. My apprentice partner and I would start at nine AM and not finish until some time between eleven PM and midnight – we got a thirty minute break around five PM on one day. There were usually five or six apprentices doing the work that the two of us were doing.

As it turns out, the weed in the woman's name probably has more to do with the amount of pot she smokes than parsley, sage, rosemary or thyme, which is something else that I would have chosen to not be around had I known.

She also failed to mention on her website and during the phone intake that she has Asperger's Syndrome (some cases are more extreme and difficult, she fell into this category) and if it were not for my young apprentice partner Liz, who was scared to death of our new "teacher", I would have left on the first day. Bizzare is an understatement of what we were living with there. Within our first couple of nights, we removed two wolf spiders almost the size of my hand from our mold, dirt, web and bug infested living quarters and on our first night we were visited by a snake about two and a half feet long. Liz almost stepped on it as she was making her way to the bathroom and screamed. I tried to catch it but it was too fast and disappeared into the wall…holes and cracks everywhere.

Our first day we only got breakfast because we went up to the house and mentioned that we did not have any food; we were given a box of stale crackers, eggs, moldy bread and goat yoghurt and milk – no lunch that day. The days following, we only got lunch to take with us during our goat watch because I demanded it; goat cheese, more stale crackers and some very old olives.

All the goat dairy was causing a real mucus problem with me – I had not had any dairy in many years and I was forced to eat a "no-thank-you-sized" portion of fish one night. I'm a vegan. Interestingly though, there was such a pervasive calmness present and alive within me while all of this was taking place that nothing seemed to rattle me. I would lay down at night and snuggle deeply into my sleeping bag (after checking for spiders and snakes) with every ounce of my being aching of exhaustion and I could not find a place inside me that felt upset, bad or sad about any of it. As a matter of fact, there was a sense of resting and being held in the arms of a loving and nurturing universe. Even after only a few hours of sleep, I would get up in the morning to begin another

150

seemingly insane day and have a smile in my heart and a feeling of exhilaration for being graced with another day of life.

Still, it was not an easy undertaking for anyone who was participating in the offerings of this teacher. I was talking with a woman from Peru who had done some workshops with this woman in the past – four in the last eighteen and twenty years and she said she had never experienced her like this. She was totally shocked at the way our teacher screamed at us and at her. I discovered later that many other participants left after my departure.

Wandering in the woods with the goats (we watched eight of them for five to six hours a day on fifty unfenced wooded acres), a wave came over me that said 'you were here for Liz to get grounded/started so she would not be alone for her first week, let go of the money and move on, it will all be okay'. Then a feeling of complete Peace came over me. I checked with my inner guidance that night before bed and got that it was time to leave. Another thing I had noticed in the woods was the opportunity to work with Liz and give her some exercises to connect with her inner power, inner guidance, her breath and heart. It was beautiful to see her taking it in and to see her grasping the techniques so quickly.

The next confirmation from the universe was when I called the person who was going to be housing me while I worked in the Boston area to see if I could come five weeks earlier. When I got him on the phone and he said "Where do you think I am right now?" He was pulling into Saugerties, NY (which is where I was) for some work that weekend with a dance company and was heading back the next day. His home is almost four hours from where I was staying in NY and he just happened to be in the neighborhood? That was definitely a thumbs-up from the universe for making the *right* decision at the perfect moment. All guidance is there when I listen.

One more interesting thing I noticed about my new way of being here; our teacher could not get *in*. I don't know if she was trying to scare me, to break me, or to shake me but none of it touched me. I am not sure if it was her Shamanic teaching or symptoms of the Asperger's Syndrome that underlay her actions but there was no fear or anxiety while I stood there with her face in my face screaming like a banshee and spit flying everywhere. I felt love as I looked in her eyes, love like when I look at the trees and other things in nature and I am pretty certain that it was showing up as a smile on my face. I left the next day.

Arriving in the Boston area, I spent five weeks visiting with family and working with clients and students from the practice that I had left behind when I moved. Everything was so different for me. Visiting with my children and siblings was such a joy. Where previously my mind would be analyzing and judging how well they were all doing, having expectations and disappointments, this visit was experienced from an open heart and a quiet mind. I just felt love – truly unconditional – and from that place came total acceptance with no effort; a complete resting in the arms of Life and 'what is'.

Many clients and students asked me during that visit what had happened to me and still others commented on the peace that was exuding from my being and the light emanating from deep within my eyes. I didn't know how to answer or how to explain to them that it was the smallest of movement that took place, a tiny shift that altered my world. Words…

The Fall

I once saw a leaf
Its graceful flight into the unknown
Flying free from its home

Not seeking to the future
Nor clinging to the past
Dancing in the moment

I watched its wild ride on the cool wind
Caressed by the warmth of the sun
Flitting by and touching the evergreen

Swirling in the scent of a rose
Before its soft landing in a stream
Joining others

In the many turns
Of the labyrinth's current
On a journey to a new world

And I understood letting go.

> *"Accepting means you allow yourself to feel whatever it is you are feeling at that moment. It is part of the is-ness of the NOW. You can't argue with what is. Well, you can, but if you do, you will suffer."* ~ Eckhart Tolle

Is my life perfect today? The answer from the divine-perspective would be yes, however, from the world's-perspective, the answer is an unequivocal no. I continue to have challenges and emotions. I still see pieces of the ego surface from time to time. The difference today is that I accept it all as perfect, even when it doesn't feel good. There is freedom from identification with my past, a relinquishment of sorts. It's beautiful to be conscious of everything as it appears and allow it to be there; to actually take it right into my heart but not have it own me in any way. Love seems to dissolve or transform all the pieces that no longer fit who I am.

It is amazing to be so alive in this body. What a gift. Today I can't imagine missing one moment of this sweet gift of Life…so precious. Awareness has expanded so much at times that the local self seems like such a funny trick that I am playing on myself.

An example: I went to Mount Shasta to pick up some class supplies and on my drive there, my awareness expanded. Gradually I became aware that I Am so Big. I am all of it and nothing is moving separately from the whole and it seemed so funny to have all my attention on this "little me" driving in this little vehicle, moving around in myself and not really going anywhere at all. The joy that I was feeling was almost overwhelming. I felt like I should have a sign displayed on my vehicle: "Caution, driver under the influence of God and may be in an altered state".

This experience might be like one tiny cell humming along with focus on its duties, moving around all by itself, seeing clearly that it's separate from all the other little cells when something removes the veil and all of a sudden waking up to the massive body carrying it. All the tiny seemingly separate cells that think they're going somewhere are actually being carried by a much more immense Being. Silly example I know but it seemed to paint the picture a bit more clearly in my head.

I've had other expanded states and blissful experiences since the awakening too. Recently, as I was out walking, all of a sudden, whoosh, I entered into stillness. I had to slow my walking and breathing down because both were making too much noise in this amazing state. I continued to float down the hill where I encountered three deer, a mother and her young ones. As we all stopped and our eyes met, instantly my heart became an inferno. The tears streamed down my cheeks and the love I felt could have consumed me whole and left behind just a pile of ashes as far as I was concerned. I was frozen in place with them for what felt like eternity but must have only been minutes.

My older brother in the VA home came to mind. Years ago as I was relaying a story to him about seeing some deer on a trail while I was out jogging, he said,

"If you could sit in their hearts you would know something," and that's what it felt like – although I'm not sure if I was sitting in their hearts or if they were sitting in mine –we were all in the One Heart I suppose.

There is a difference today with the way I feel after the *spiritual experiences* pass. Previously, I would search for more, long to be there again, examine my surroundings and make mental notes so I could recreate it. In some cases, depression would set in for days or weeks. Today, I marvel at them, fully accept their comings and goings and no longer need to have more close-encounters to be full.

Such staggering Love; it keeps bubbling up and spilling over, sometimes almost into giggles as it's too big to contain. My heart just wants to hug everyone, my mouth just wants to say I love you, and instead I stand there with a giddy grin on my face.

One last point...

Most of us in this very confused country (world) have been wired to think that just because we feel deep love, intense love, breathtaking love, that it means we are "in love" and the next natural move would be sexual intimacy. While there is nothing wrong with sexual intimacy (it can be such an incredibly beautiful experience that enlivens the soul!), once we find that Love resides in us, as us, we will never need someone else to provide it for us. There is no void to fill and all aspects of relationships become so much richer. You are Love, truly that's all there is. When we can get to the other side of our judgments about what Life is and the story of what happened to *me*, we land in Love.

Thank you God for life experiences, for my teachers and the whole divine plan – I bow to You with such gratitude and Love; words cannot express what I feel; unbound comes to mind; free. This is Love that is unbound by concepts, beliefs, wishes – no limits. Everything in Life feels like a YES. Each thing is so new, like the first time I've ever really experienced it. I've been here but never Here. It's hard to tell where I end and the *other* begins.

This infinite love is what we are up to here. It is what we came to experience…for all beings… and what is really amazing is when we find it in the self, the heart shatters into a dimension that is unfathomable by the mind and love without limits is experienced.

Like a baby experiencing the world for the first time, when here, truly here, completely and fully here, life can be really breath-taking.

God's Wings

Kayaking at Field pond

State forest

Sweet love filled the air

Filled my heart

And carried me about

As I made the motions of paddling

God's wings carried me to such beautiful expressions

of Life.

The geese came together, gathering, honking

One by one, rounding up the others with their calls

My heart was touched when I discovered they were

not just saying hello

But protecting the nest

All of them

Together

As One.

Drifting in love, moving in grace

The turtle saw us

The camera

And she posed with assurance

And posed

She let us get so close

Then one last pose before her dive amongst the

bursting water lilies.

All so magnificent, so splendid

But the great blue heron stole the show as she teased

Dipped and hid, and then took flight again and again

With my heart on her wings

She carried me to You

And through You God, to me...

Beloved.

God, Life is beautiful.

Dive into the mystery of the present moment; look for

the gem in every situation. New life, grander

perspective and sweet beginnings are most often

disguised as painful endings. Don't be fooled. Life is

a gift. Hang in there for the miracle, even if you're not expecting one.

Visit the website for a calendar of events at:

www.shelleerae.com

Invite the author to your area by contacting her at:

shelleerae@shelleerae.com

Made in United States
Troutdale, OR
10/13/2023